Hello Lucas

A Life-Transforming Journey
Through the Teachings of Jesus

DANIEL F. HURT

ILLUMIFY
MEDIA.COM

Published by
Illumify Media Global
www.IllumifyMedia.com
"Let's bring your book to life!"

Library of Congress Control Number: 2025906302

Paperback ISBN: 978-1-964251-63-9

Cover design by Debbie Lewis

Printed in the United States of America

Contents

Introduction

I stared through the dusty windshield of my old Dodge Charger toward the main office of the junkyard, patiently waiting for it to open. As I went over a mental list of the used parts I needed, the deep, rhythmic rumble of a motorcycle caught my attention. On an extremely well-kept, collectible British motorcycle sat a tough- and lean-looking biker, lounged and laid back. He was dressed in jeans, boots, leather jacket, and all. His black, waist-length hair gently moved in the breeze and mingled with the cigarette smoke meandering from his mouth. To my young, twenty-one-year-old, impressionable mind, everything about his presentation communicated loudly, *I am the essence of cool.*

The more I looked on, the more I was drawn to ponder deeply, *I wonder if a man so filled with pride and, yes, even arrogance might be prepared to meet the Lord were he to wreck that bike and not survive.* The awe and mystique that surrounded him faded into concern and compassion. *I need to talk to him about the Lord,* I thought.

That quick, I opened my door and headed straight toward him. From a distance I could see him watching, a bit like a wolf waiting to respond if I made the wrong move. It didn't take me long to reach him and begin sharing a condensed version of the Gospel. When I finished, he looked down at me and said in the most condescending tone, "Get the hell away from me."

I said, "Okay. Just know this, God loves you."

After finishing my business, I left the junkyard and spent the next several years praying for that man as he would come to mind.

One day, when I was visiting a town four hours from my home, I stopped into a local church for the evening meeting. After enjoying a nice service, I headed for the door.

One of the members interrupted me. "Hi, I'm Leroy," he said. "Do you remember me?"

"I'm sorry, I don't," I replied.

"I'm the guy that was on the motorcycle," he said. "I've given my life to Jesus Christ, and I want to thank you for sharing the Gospel with me."

I was speechless, pleasantly dumbfounded at the power of the Gospel to convert someone who was so at odds with God. What stood before me now was a man obviously changed by the Spirit of God. Most of his physical features were the same, though a little more groomed. But his personality radiated kindness and gentleness. We spent a short time rejoicing and reminiscing before I went on my way.

For as long as I can remember, wherever I have gone around the world, I have felt comfortable sharing the good news of Jesus Christ with other people. And whenever I do, quite often they respond by giving their life to the Lord right then and there. They choose to turn to God and away from all that offends Him and to put their faith in Jesus, accepting all that He purchased for them through His life, suffering, and resurrection. One of the greatest joys in my life is being a part of that experience, when a person who is unclear about God finally encounters and receives the overwhelming love that He has for them.

Most of my life I was content to randomly meet people, introduce them to their beloved Savior, lead them in a prayer committing to that relationship, and then be on my way. Because most of the people I met were complete strangers, I never saw them again. There was no exchanging of phone numbers or addresses, no follow-up discussion or training to help them in their newfound faith. It was much like a woman giving birth to a baby, placing the child in a crib with diapers and a bottle of milk, then saying, "I've done the hard part; now you must take care of yourself." All of that changed when I met Lucas.

My wife and I have a lifelong commitment to global evangelism and missions work through our ministry, Fire Around the World, which has continued for thirty years. In order to take care of our family needs, my wife worked as a senior accountant, and I as a general construction contractor. In addition to all that, we constructed or completely remodeled another fourteen single-dwelling residential units within a fifteen-year period. We were exhausted and finally retired from our secular employment. However, we found ourselves in another construction project, building our dream home atop an 8,500-foot mountain range in northern Colorado.

It was there, two years before the writing of this book, during that construction project, that we first met Lucas. He arrived as a subcontractor, appointed to oversee and execute the electrical work on our cabin. Within minutes of introductions, I felt a tangible presence of the love of God for him. It was a gift from God to experience the emotions of God for someone who was previously unknown to me. Recognizing the heart of God, I immediately shared the Gospel, which Lucas gladly received with faith and obedience. And like before, that probably would have been the end of my spiritual involvement, but God had different ideas and would speak to me through His Word.

In my daily reading of the Word, the Holy Spirit quickly drew my heart to read and ponder on Matthew chapter seven. The particular passage that spoke to me was Matthew 7:21-24, where Jesus said, "Not everyone who says to me, 'Lord, Lord,' will enter the kingdom of heaven, but only the one who does the will of my Father who is in heaven. Many will say to me on that day, 'Lord, Lord, did we not prophesy in your name and in your name drive out demons and in your name perform many miracles?' Then I will tell them plainly, 'I never knew you. Away from me, you evildoers!' Therefore everyone who hears these words of mine and puts them into practice is like a wise man who built his house on the rock."

As I read this passage, I was shaken to the core. Throughout my years of foreign missions, I had cast out demons regularly and seen countless miracles. Those who were blind, mute, and paralyzed from birth were healed; even one dead girl was raised to life when we prayed for her in Jesus's name. But now I was feeling a deep, indescribable sense of inadequacy; or was it insecurity? I couldn't distinguish. Somehow the specifics didn't matter. All I knew was that I could not for a single moment rest my confidence in the fact that I had preached a good sermon or had miraculous signs accompanying my ministry or missions work. This fresh revelation overwhelmed me. God was revealing His heart to me, and I wanted to drink in every thought of it and every word that Jesus said until His heart's desires became my heart's desires.

I must know, take to heart, and obey the teachings of Jesus in every level of my life. To love Him is to know and do His Word. Just as the physical body is inseparable from the heart, He is inseparable from His Word. I cannot say that I love Him and refuse to do as He teaches.

The apostle John said it this way:

> In the beginning was the Word, and the Word was with God, and the Word was God. He was with God in the beginning. Through him all things were made; without him nothing was made that has been made. . . . The Word became flesh and made his dwelling among us. We have seen his glory, the glory of the one and only Son, who came from the Father, full of grace and truth. (John 1:1-3, 14)

Imagine that. God wanted to reveal the full content of His heart to you, every thought, every desire, His passion and intimate feelings for you, what drives Him, what makes Him tick. Every word that He wanted to speak to you personally, He chose to embed within the very DNA of His Son, so that it could be personally delivered to you. That's why Jesus said, "These words you hear are not my own; they belong to the Father who sent me" (John 14:24).

I felt an urgency to somehow convey this truth to Lucas. I was determined from then on that whomever I led to Jesus must clearly understand this as well. To love Jesus is to love and do His Word. My responsibility was clear: to impart the teachings of Jesus to new believers. But how could I do this in a practical sense for Lucas? I wouldn't be around to lead him in a Bible study. Our lifestyle of travel and ministry makes it impossible for us to even have pets. If we can't give pets proper care and attention, how could I ever attend to Lucas's development?

I did not have to think about it for long before the Lord gave me the solution. I was to contact Lucas and share with him the importance of what I had learned. Since the words of Jesus are contained mainly in the four Gospels and Acts, he would start in Matthew, reading half a chapter a day and continue through Mark, Luke, John, and the book of Acts. Each day I would send a short phone text explaining the passages that he had read. God told me specifically that I was not to ask him if he would participate, rather just lead him in this step forward. He would not be obligated to reply but could if he had questions. It was the perfect solution. He would have the liberty to follow along without the undue burden of talking to me every day. And I had the flexibility to disciple him from any country that I found myself in.

This system of reading and texting continued successfully with him every day for over a year until we completed the book of Acts. I moved forward using this system with every new person whom I led to Jesus. At one point, I was juggling fifteen people daily through different Bible passages. For smaller groups of disciples, this method worked great, but as the number grew, it became impractical to keep up with. As a result, the Lord led me to publish these texts and put a printed version in the hands of every new believer. Within this text, I have attempted to place a solid foundation for Lucas and any new believer to build upon. I have been faithful to Jesus's command: "Therefore go and make disciples of all nations, baptizing them in the name of the Father and of the Son and of the Holy Spirit, and teaching them to obey everything I have commanded you" (Matthew 28:19–20).

Have you ever led someone to Christ but not felt comfortable taking them deeper? Is there someone you know who is asking questions about God, and you don't know how to respond? The best place to start is with the teachings of Jesus. Give them a copy of this book as a practical guide to help them on their journey through the Gospels. Possibly you have given your life to Jesus Christ and have never been discipled in the teachings of Jesus. Maybe you have browsed the multitude of Biblical messages and conflicting comments that abound on social media but have never taken time to read and make an honest effort to apply the teachings of Jesus to your personal life. No one can live the Christian life for you. The fruit of your spiritual life will ultimately be a product of your own relationship and obedience to the teachings of Jesus. Now's your chance. I welcome you to follow along with Lucas on this brief but powerful daily adventure.

Be blessed.

CHAPTER ONE

Letters to Lucas

Tuesday, June 22, 2021—7:20 a.m.

Hello Lucas,

I wanted to encourage you as you grow in your knowledge and love for the Lord. As you know, we need daily food for our bodies to survive. Likewise, our spirit man needs daily food, which is God's Word. Remember that I mentioned for you to begin in Matthew and read on from there? Each day I'll try to send a text message like this to comment on the day's Bible passage, don't feel obligated to reply, but if you have questions, feel free to ask.

Blessings, Brother.

Wednesday, June 23, 2021

Hello Lucas,

As we go through the teachings of Jesus, it's not only important that you read them, you must act upon them also. As you read His words, ask yourself, "What did Jesus just say, and how does that apply to me?" Then live it out in a practical day-to-day lifestyle. Simply put, read the Word and then do what it says.

James, the half brother of Jesus, said it this way: "Do not merely listen to the word, and so deceive yourselves. Do what it says. Anyone who listens to the word but does not do what it says is like someone who looks at his face in a mirror and, after looking at himself, goes away and immediately forgets what he looks like" (James 1:22–24).

Here, James is telling us that the man who hears the teachings of Jesus but does not do them is being deceived by himself. That person looks into the Word much like one standing in front of a spiritual mirror. He sees his condition and issues but refuses to acknowledge them, or he makes excuses about his situation. Maybe he thinks of how that Word applies to others but not himself. In doing so, he never makes a practical application of Jesus's commands to his own life.

Because he does not act on the Word, nothing inside him changes. His old nature is never subdued long enough for the divine characteristics of God to grow within him. When he steps away from the mirror of the Word and goes about his life, he does not know how he will react to situations or temptations in life. Because he is not obeying the teachings of Christ, he just reacts as his old impulses drive him.

All along, he feels spiritually confident because he has fulfilled his religious duty of reading God's Word. That man is living a self-deceived life. He does not have new life in Christ and is actually spiritually dead. Make sure that you are not like that man.

Blessings, Brother.

3

Thursday, June 24, 2021

Hello Lucas,

You have come to know the love that God has for you, and you have put your faith in Jesus Christ, His one and only Son.

People put their faith in God for many different reasons. Some have searched for truth their whole lives; some have lost everything in life; some developed health issues that threatened their lives. Others have never experienced true love; some hit the bottom of the barrel or were looking for freedom from addiction. Some were opposing God and running from Him, and some were just ready to give up completely by ending their lives. Whatever the reason, they finally ended up in the arms of their loving heavenly Father. They received the answers and solutions that they needed from the one who knows them best. As a result, they have put their full faith and confidence in Him.

My wife and I minister extensively across India, and one of the stories that we hear over and over goes like this:

> I was blind my whole life, sitting in my village. Many animal sacrifices were made for me, and many offerings given to the priests. Endless prayers were made for my healing. I have visited many hospitals and spent much money and all of this without cure. All the people in this village know me as that man. But when I was prayed for in the name of Jesus Christ, my eyes were healed! So now I am giving my life to Jesus Christ and putting my faith in the true and living God. (Elderly blind man from the Miji tribe, Nafra village, Arunachal Pradesh)

Like this man, every year, all across India, thousands put their faith in God because He is healing their bodies. All around the world, God is graciously meeting people at their point of need and introducing Himself to them, and they respond by having faith in Him. That type of introductory faith is amazing. It's our personal experience and testimony to God's faithfulness in meeting our felt needs in life. It is a powerful reason to put faith in God, and no one can refute your personal story.

Besides your personal experience, has God given you other substantial evidence so that you can have unshakable faith in Him and His Word? We'll look at that question tomorrow.

Blessings, Brother.

Friday, June 25, 2021

Hello Lucas,

Soon you will begin reading the Gospel of Matthew and be expected to take to heart the teachings of Jesus. In order to accomplish that goal, you must have the highest confidence and faith that God is real and that his Word is true. You believe now because you have heard about and experienced the love that God has for you. But what evidence did God lay out ahead of time so that you can have complete confidence and faith in His Word, this book we call the Bible?

Have you ever heard someone say, "You've just got to have faith in God"? It sounds as though you must believe in someone's thin idea without a bit of evidence. Imagine this: You go to a friend's house for dinner. He welcomes you in and says, "Hang your coat and hat over there on the wall, so we can enjoy the time." You look, but there is no nail or hook, just a smooth wall. You would agree with me; there must be something solid to hang your hat on. Your new life in Christ is the same way. You have entered the house and family of God. There must be something solid to hang your faith on, so you can relax and have fellowship with Him And for sure, He has already provided many solid "hooks" of evidence, so you can have unshakable faith in Him and His Word. Let's take a look at the first one.

#1. Nature itself declares that there must be a Creator God.

King David said it this way: "The heavens declare the glory of God; the skies proclaim the work of his hands," (Psalm 19:1). The same principle was used by the founding fathers of America when they wrote in the Declaration of Independence, "We hold these truths to be self-evident." They were saying that some things in life are obvious by the evidence that surrounds them, and that using a little common sense will reveal those simple truths

Many years ago, I was traveling the jungle roads of the Himalayan Mountains that separate Northeast India and southern China. In this remote area, around 13,700 feet high, I came upon a stone house. It was standing alone in a desolate area with no one around. Being a builder myself, I examined it closely. It was stone laid upon stone, made of large and tiny rocks perfectly fitted together without the use of any type of mortar, mud, or cement, yet so tightly fitted that air could not pass through. Absolutely nothing in it was manufactured; everything was made of natural and organic material. It was perfectly square and level.

As I marveled at its beauty, the thought never entered my mind that this building happened by accident or developed through some evolutionary rock-formation process. It was self-evident that there was a builder for this structure. Common sense said to me, *This is constructed in such a magnificent way, that if I should ever meet the builder, I would like to congratulate him*. And so it is with God. His creation declares His existence, and He is to be congratulated and trusted.

Tomorrow we will look at a second solid "hook" of evidence that we can rest our faith upon.

Blessings, Brother.

Saturday, June 26, 2021

Hello Lucas,

Let's look today at the second evidence that God gave so we can rest in faith.

#2. God's Word is based upon prophecy.

One fourth of all the Bible is prophecy. That's one in every four verses. There are about 2,500 prophecies and around 2,000 have already been fulfilled specifically and in detail. The claims of Jesus Christ being the Son of God was authenticated by the hundreds of prophesies that were historically fulfilled during his birth, life, death, and resurrection. The mathematical odds of these things happening are astronomical, and many notable mathematicians have written documents regarding that fact. No other writing, no other religion has that volume of verifiable evidence. There's a certain small amount of prophecy in other religious writing and secular fortune tellers, but it's usually general in scope and can apply to several different situations, whereas the Bible is very specific in its details of locations and events, which makes it much easier to validate historically. God speaks clearly about His uniqueness regarding this evidence of prophetic foretelling. "Remember the former things, those of long ago; I am God, and there is no other; I am God, and there is none like me. I make known the end from the beginning, from ancient times, what is still to come," (Isaiah 46:9–10). The thing that distinguishes God and verifies His Word is this: He foretells events so that people can fact check and conclude that He has told the truth. We can rest assured in faith that His Word is true—past, present, and future.

Tomorrow we will look at a third solid "hook" of evidence that you can rest your faith upon.

Blessings, Brother.

Hello Lucas,

Let's look today at the third evidence that God gave so that we can rest in faith.

#3. Jesus chose twelve eyewitnesses.

There are an estimated ten thousand distinct religions worldwide. In fact, it seems that people around the world continue to create new gods for almost everything imaginable. One year when I was in Nepal, I met with a Buddhist priest at the Buddha Stupa in Kathmandu. He showed me various alcoves filled with statues of gods.

As he explained their attributes and purposes, I spotted one empty shelf, so I asked him, "Why is that place missing it's god?"

He replied, "Now that technology exists, we are creating a new god to rule over technology. His image is not finished yet."

With so many religions and gods, how do we know that Jesus is truly God and that the others are invented by men? And what about Jesus's claim: "I am the way and the truth and the life. No one comes to the Father except through me" (John 14:6)? In another place He said, "All who have come before me are thieves and robbers. . . . I am the gate; whoever enters through me will be saved" (John 10:8–9).

To find the answer, we must consider the legal validity of anyone's singular account. One man's testimony alone does not carry enough weight to establish a case. There must be evidence presented by additional witnesses. Anyone can claim having an enlightened spiritual experience, a supernatural encounter with heavenly beings, or having received new revelation or updated words from God. But without solid collaboration, these individual claims are meritless. Jesus openly used this very principle as a guideline for himself. When speaking to the religious leaders of His day, He said, "If I testify about myself, my testimony is not true. . . . these are the very Scriptures that testify about me" (John 5:31, 39).

Before Jesus appeared, God chose many prophets as witnesses to foretell the most intimate details of the coming Messiah. Then He selected twelve men (the disciples) to accompany Jesus as witnesses during His three and a half years of public ministry, His death, and His resurrection. In a court of law, certainly three eyewitnesses could establish a case beyond a reasonable doubt. However, God in His extravagance has provided many more than that.

Seventy-eight percent of the world's population adhere to four main religions: Christianity (32%), Islam (24%), Hinduism (15%), and Buddhism (7%). Out of these four, three are based upon the experience and singular testimony of their founders without solid collaboration. Christianity alone rests upon the testimonies of scores of witnesses who, by the way, held to their testimony even when threatened by death. We have faith in Jesus because of the witnesses God has provided.

We have faith in God because it is self-evident from observing our natural world that there is a Creator God. We have faith in God's Word because it is validated through the multitude of verifiable prophesies. We have faith in who Jesus is and what He said because of the testimonies of the many eyewitnesses who agree.

Blessings, Brother.

Monday, June 28, 2021

Hello Lucas,

Tomorrow you will begin reading the teachings of Jesus as recorded in the four Gospels and the book of Acts from the Bible. Jesus's life, words, and teachings were originally written on five different scrolls, as recorded by five different writers. Since these men were giving their account of the same events, you will notice some of the stories are repeated as you read the various books. Each of the authors are describing the events as viewed through their different eyes. The facts remain the same, but the writers notice and emphasize different points.

According to researchers, the New Testament has been preserved in more manuscripts than any other ancient work of literature, with over twenty-five thousand complete or fragmented manuscripts catalogued to date. The oldest known manuscript is excerpted from the Gospel of John and dated around AD 150. The apostle John died around AD 99, so it is within fifty years of his life.

Let's look briefly at each book and author that you will be reading:

1. The Gospel of Matthew

Matthew's Theme: Jesus the coming Messiah, Son of David, and King

Matthew was one of the twelve apostles chosen by Jesus, and most ancient manuscripts credit him as the author of this gospel. In his account, Matthew uses at least twenty-nine different prophesies to show that Jesus is not just a new religious figure creating a new religion. Rather, He is the fulfillment of God's Old Testament prophesies.

2. The Gospel of Mark

Mark's Theme: Jesus the Servant

Mark, properly named John Mark, was the son of a widow woman and the cousin of Barnabas. He helped Peter, Barnabas, and Paul in the ministry. He was one of the followers of Jesus, and the early church credited him as the author of this gospel.

3. The Gospel of Luke

Luke's Theme: Jesus the Son of Man

Luke was a well-educated doctor and believed by many to have been a Greek. He traveled extensively, ministering with Paul, and is generally credited as the author. If so, he would be the only non-Jewish writer of a book of the Bible.

He says that he was led by God to interview eyewitnesses and write an orderly account of Jesus's life for a new believer named Theophilus.

4. The Gospel of John

John's Theme: Jesus the Son of God

John was one of the twelve apostles chosen by Jesus and an eyewitness to all that Jesus said and did. Even though the Gospel of John refers to John as "the one whom Jesus loved," the early church credits John himself as the author.

5. The Book of Acts

Acts' Theme: Jesus's work continued through the church as empowered by the Holy Spirit.

The Holy Spirit is mentioned seventy times. The word *power* is used twenty-five times. And the word *witness* is used over thirty times in this book. Church tradition and many scholars identify Luke as the author of Acts. Acts, like the Gospel of Luke, is addressed to a new believer named Theophilus.

Blessings, Brother.

CHAPTER TWO

Matthew

Day One

Matthew 1:1–17

Hello Lucas,

As you begin each day, just read the scriptures listed above, then read my text afterward.

Matthew opens up his gospel by linking the genealogy of Jesus to three previous events, each occurring approximately fourteen generations apart. In doing so, he traces the lineage of Jesus through his adoptive father, Joseph, and through King David to Abraham, who was the father of the Jewish nation.

But what is the significance of the three events that are described as being approximately "fourteen generations apart," and why are they brought to our attention? Each of the events mentioned is connected to its own ancient prophecy, and each prophecy reveals its own unique detail about the lineage and coming of the Christ. Let's look closer at the three events and prophesies that foretold Jesus's coming.

#1 Ancient Prophecy: The Messiah/Christ would come from Abraham's lineage.

Genesis 22:18 says, "Through your offspring all nations on earth will be blessed, because you have obeyed me."

(Fourteen generations from Abraham to King David)

#2 Ancient Prophecy: The Messiah/Christ would come from King David's lineage.

2 Samuel 7:12–13 says, "When your days are over and you rest with your ancestors, I will raise up your offspring to succeed you, your own flesh and blood, and I will establish his kingdom. He is the one who will build a house for my Name, and I will establish the throne of his kingdom forever."

(Fourteen generations from King David to the Babylonian captivity)

#3 Ancient Prophecy: The Messiah/Christ would come after Israels captivity in Babylon.

Jeremiah 23:5–6 says, " 'The days are coming,' declares the LORD, 'when I will raise up for David a righteous Branch, a King who will reign wisely and do what is just and right in the land. In his days Judah will be saved and Israel will live in safety. This is the name by which he will be called: The LORD Our Righteous Savior."

(Fourteen generations from the Babylonian captivity to the birth of Christ)

All three ancient prophesies were fulfilled by the birth and lineage of Jesus Christ. It was God's plan all along that Jesus would be conceived by the Holy Spirit and not by man. Matthew is telling us clearly that through the adoption process, Jesus became Joseph's heir, and that His birth legally fulfilled each one of the ancient prophesies just as God had planned Son of Abraham, Son of David, and born after the captivity in Babylon.

Blessings. Have a great day.

Day Two

Matthew 1:18–25

Hello Lucas,

From the beginning of time, God has spoken through the prophets, describing every detail of how He would send His Son—the village He would be born in, that He would be born of a virgin, the details of His family line, how He would die—every detail.

Three hundred specific prophesies were fulfilled by Jesus. Matthew is describing some of these fulfilled prophesies so that you can know that Jesus was sent from God.

Blessings. Have a great day.

Day Three

Matthew 2:1–12

Hello Lucas,

When Jesus was born, Israel was occupied and ruled by Rome. Herod, the regional king, learned from the three wise men that the "king of the Jews" had been born, so he tried to find and kill baby Jesus.

Satan knows that it is easier to kill a baby than to conquer a king. It is the same with us. When you accept Jesus, you are a baby Christian. The devil will try to bring people into your life to kill your walk with God. Some people will reject you; some will try to tempt you and lure you away from your new love for God.

God will show you the safe way through each situation so that you can grow into a strong man of God.

Blessings. Have a great day.

Day Four

Matthew 2:13–23

Hello Lucas,

Matthew gives four more ancient prophesies about Jesus's coming that played out through the events surrounding His birth and early adolescent years. Even though Jesus was a baby and unable to manipulate the circumstances to fit the prophesies, these things happened just the way God had foretold. Here are the four prophesies:

1. Verse 5—He would be born in the city of Bethlehem in the region of Judea (spoken by the prophet Micah 698 to 740 years earlier).
2. Verse 15—God would call His son out of Egypt (spoken by the prophet Hosea 746 to 786 years earlier).
3. Verse 18—Israeli children would be slaughtered near Rachel's tomb, and unconsolable weeping would take place (spoken by Jeremiah the prophet 580 to 626 years earlier).
4. Verse 23—Jesus would come from the region of Galilee, hence the town of Nazareth (spoken by the prophet Isaiah 701 to 740 years earlier).

Blessings. Have a great day.

Day Five

Matthew 3:1–12

Hello Lucas,

Around seven hundred years before Jesus came, Isaiah prophesied that God would send a messenger ahead of Christ to prepare the people's hearts to receive Him. That messenger was John the Baptist. John prepared the way by preaching the truth and telling people to repent (turn away from their sins and turn to God). Thousands of people came out to hear him and openly admitted their sins in front of everyone and then were baptized.

John baptized his followers in water, which symbolizes the washing away of your sins, the burial of your old sinful man, and being raised up to live a new life. He also told the people that the promised Messiah (Jesus) would come and baptize them with the Holy Spirit and fire, which represents the Holy Spirit living within you as a refining fire. Much like the gold refiner, the Holy Spirit burns within your personal life, bringing all your impurities to the surface so they can be removed.

As you grow in the Lord, the Holy Spirit will bring your impurities to the surface for you to see. Don't be discouraged by this cleansing work of God. Learn to cooperate with the work of the Holy Spirit, and your life will shine brighter than the purest gold.

Blessings. Have a great day.

Day Six

Matthew 3:13–17

Hello Lucas,

When Jesus came to the river to be baptized by John, God spoke out loud from heaven telling the people, "This is my Son, whom I love; with him I am well pleased" (Matthew 3:17), and the Holy Spirit rested on Him like a dove. Now John knew without a doubt that Jesus was the Messiah, and from that time on, he pointed everyone to Him. John's job as waymaker and forerunner was almost completed. Public attention for him would decrease, and Jesus's ministry would come to the forefront.

Like John, your life should be lived in such a way that you fulfill the purposes of God for your generation. When you do that effectively, amazing things will happen, miracles will occur, great things will be accomplished, and to some people you will look like a powerful man of God. When that happens, never let yourself get caught up in the moment. Your success and elevation have come for the glory of God and the advancement of His Kingdom. Never let it become about you, your success, or your ministry. If you do, you will be stealing God's glory, and it will be your downfall. People's eyes will be on you instead of Jesus, and if you stumble, many others will fall. Instead, always let Jesus be in the forefront and let your life be a signpost pointing everyone you meet to Him.

Blessings. Have a great day.

Day Seven

Matthew 4:1–11

Hello Lucas,

Jesus was with God in the beginning. He temporarily set aside His position and authority and took on a human body. As a human, He had to be tempted in every way like us but without sinning. That made it possible for Him to offer His sinless blood and body as payment for your sins. That is why He often referred to Himself as "the Son of Man." As human, He relied on the help of the Holy Spirit to lead Him through this. Notice that He quoted scriptures that related to each temptation.

Here are three powerful tools that you have been given that will help you win over temptation.

1. Jesus is your sympathetic high priest. He was tempted like you and understands your struggle. You can come to Him boldly and honestly with your sins and issues. He is your representative and is already speaking to God about your situation.
2. The Holy Spirit is your helper and is working within you. He is the one who is dealing with your conscience, bringing scriptures to your mind, and showing you how to overcome. Learn to recognize His gentle presence within and cooperate with His leading.
3. Do like Jesus did. Memorize a Bible verse that speaks about your temptation and speak it out loud. That's why the Word of God is called the sword of the Spirit. It will defeat the enemy and the temptation.

Blessings. Have a great day.

Day Eight

Matthew 4:12–25

Hello Lucas,

Matthew continues to show how Jesus's life fulfilled prophesies.

Now Jesus begins his public ministry, which only lasts about three years but turns the entire world upside down.

Look at the love and devotion of His followers. John the Baptist is imprisoned and beheaded for preaching repentance. When Jesus calls the disciples, they leave everything to follow Him.

When God calls you, you realize that this world is temporary, and that your real home is in heaven. He may not ask you to leave everything you have. But now in your heart, these things no longer have the importance they used to. Heavenly things and your relationship with God become your first love. Lucas, as you grow in your understanding of that, you will find great contentment and peace in this world, and you will store up for yourself great treasures in heaven.

Blessings. Have a great day.

Day Nine

Matthew 5:1–16

Hello Lucas,

Large crowds of people followed Jesus because they saw the amazing healing miracles that He was doing. He sat down on a mountain and taught what living in the kingdom of God is like, how to have God's blessings rest on you, and how you should live. Often people around us live as though there are no consequences or benefits that result from their actions. They are just living for the moment, impulsively doing and saying whatever comes to mind. But here Jesus is teaching the people that every earthly action is actually a heavenly transaction. How you live on earth brings about a corresponding response from God.

This is what He promises you:

1. If you realize how poor your spiritual condition is, God will open His kingdom to you.
2. If you are broken and grieving, God will send you comfort.
3. If you walk humbly now, you will rule with Jesus on this earth when He returns.
4. If you truly hunger for what is right and to be righteous, God will fill your life with that.
5. If you are merciful and compassionate to others, God will have mercy on you.
6. If you keep your heart clean and pure, you will get to see God.
7. If you are a peacemaker, you will be recognized as one of God's sons.
8. If you are persecuted for being righteous and doing right, God will open His kingdom to you.
9. If people defame and persecute you for being a Christian, God will reward you greatly in heaven.

Blessings. Have a great day.

Day Ten

Matthew 5:17–48

Hello Lucas,

The religious leaders of that day didn't understand the Ten Commandments and the law, and they had forced their own ideas and requirements on the crowd. So Jesus went through the commandments one by one, explaining what God meant and showing that it is possible to read a commandment but miss the meaning. That is a problem called the "letter" of the law verses the "intent" or "righteousness" of the law.

Sometimes when people get into an emotional discussion, they argue over the smallest words and miss the whole point that the other person is making. That's where the saying applies, "You may have won the battle, but you lost the war." It's possible to win an argument but never understand the other person's heart.

To properly mature as a new believer, you must recognize that the commands of God merely reflect the desires of God, and that the desires of God reside within the heart of God. In fact, His commands are an invitation to look within the secret council chamber of His heart and intimately know Him. In doing so, you will not find the letter of the command. Instead you will discover the full beauty of the justice, righteousness, mercy, and love that necessitated the command. These beautiful virtues are the very essence of His being and are there waiting for you to discover. Moses said it this way: "If you are pleased with me, teach me your ways so I may know you," (Exodus 33:13).

Jesus ended His teaching by explaining that if you learn to walk in love like God does, you will automatically fulfill the law and commandments. Lucas, always walk in love. Then you will be like your heavenly Father. And never stop asking the question, "God, what is in your heart?" Then you will always know Him intimately.

Blessings. Have a great day.

Day Eleven

Matthew 6:1–4

Hello Lucas,

People do all types of religious acts and good deeds for different reasons. Some want to receive acknowledgement and praise. Others want the "favor" repaid later: "You scratch my back; I'll scratch yours." And others think that they are earning their way into heaven. God knows the motive in your heart. Here Jesus challenges you to do a heart check and adjust the things that are off. He teaches you the proper way to serve God in prayer, fasting (skipping meals), and doing good deeds for others. He says that you should not do these things to impress others. Instead, quietly, you should do them before God. Then God will reward and honor you in front of others. Again, we see that every one of your earthly actions is actually a heavenly transaction.

He teaches that your true future is in heaven and that you should not worry so much about your earthly treasures and needs. Out of all the creatures that God has created, you are the one made in His image. He values you the most, and He will take care of all your earthly needs. So don't worry; just bring your needs to Him confidently.

Blessings. Have a great day.

Day Twelve

Matthew 6:5–34

Hello Lucas,

As I have traveled around the world, I've seen people make prayers in interesting and unusual ways. One year I was at the Dalai Lama Buddhist temple in the foothills of the Dhauladhar mountain range in Northwest India. There, people would spin metal drum-shaped "prayer wheels" day and night. Later when I asked, "To whom and where do the prayers go?" they replied, "We don't know; we just do."

I have heard Hindus chant nonstop mantras. I have even heard Christians make endless prescript, liturgical prayers to the dead and use amulet beads. Most of these efforts amount to nothing more than mindless spiritual exercises that produce no results. Why? Because it is not the proper protocol for approaching God. Jesus knew that we have a tendency to turn everything spiritual into religious ritual and duty, so he taught us how to address God properly and effectively.

In the Lord's Prayer, Jesus taught us this pattern for prayer that brings results:

1. "Our Father": You have a personal relationship and are appealing to your compassionate Father. You are legally His child, and He will care for you appropriately.
2. "In Heaven": He is not just any god, but the true and living God, Creator, who is seated in heaven.
3. "Hallowed be your name": Daily, people take God's name in vain, so you declare it to be holy.
4. "Your kingdom come": Satan legally took earth's dominion from Adam, and Jesus legally won it back. He is now establishing His kingdom on earth one person at a time—established within the hearts of men.
5. "Your will be done, on earth as it is in heaven": The perfection of God's kingdom in heaven is possible because His will is carried out there. Let's see that same establishment of perfection here on earth. It begins as you allow His will to be accomplished, and your plans are no longer the focus of your life.
6. "Give us today our daily bread": You are not told to pray for your monthly or weekly bread, but daily. Every day you are in communication with Him. Every day you are fellowshipping, looking

to Him for your physical and spiritual existence. Today He will provide. Don't worry about tomorrow.

7. "Forgive us our debts, as we also have forgiven our debtors": He freely forgives your sins to the measure that you forgive others. Often it is not an enemy but those closest to you who will hurt you the most. Never hold a grudge. Let it go.

8. "Lead us not into temptation": In the past, you have lusted after many things. It is always good to ask God to create a clean heart in you and keep you from being tempted.

9. "Deliver us from the evil one": You cannot conquer evil alone; you need a deliverer. You should never take the attitude that says, "I've got this God." No matter how many victories I have had, I've learned that I cannot sustain victory over evil in my own strength. Rely on Him daily for your victory.

10. "For yours is the kingdom and the power and the glory forever. Amen": Include thanks and appreciation every time you pray. Give credit and honor to the one who answers your prayers and sustains your life.

Do not mindlessly repeat the Lord's Prayer, but use it as a pattern while speaking to God from your heart, and watch the answers pour in.

Blessings. Have a great day.

Day Thirteen

Matthew 7:1–12

Hello Lucas,

Jesus continues teaching about living properly in God's kingdom. He tells you to inspect your own heart before judging other people's situations. When your heart is clean, only then can you properly judge others.

You do not judge others in order to sentence them. You make value judgments so that you can help them be free from their sins and issues. The ultimate goal in judging is not to prosecute and bring judgment down on someone but to change their heart and save them from destruction.

If a man remains wicked, he will give account of himself to God on Judgment Day.

Blessings. Have a great day.

Day Fourteen

Matthew 7:13–29

Hello Lucas,

Here, Jesus is giving a couple of sobering reality checks for people who want to have eternal life. He describes two different situations wherein most of the people end up with eternal destruction instead. Let's look at the two scenarios:

1. There is a wide, spacious on-ramp and road with no obstacles described, like a superhighway that most people are traveling on. However, the heavenly GPS shows that their final destination is a place called Utter Destruction and Eternal Ruin. Next to it is a narrow, hard-to-maneuver road with a narrow and obstructed on-ramp, which only a few people find. The heavenly GPS shows that its final destination is a place called Eternal Life. Jesus is that narrow gate and way. Notice how He uses the words "many and few" in order to challenge your journey and destination. He starts with "Enter the narrow gate."

2. Here, Jesus warns you that there are fake Christians, fake leaders, and fake followers. They go to church, call themselves Christians, preach, and do ministry work. By all outward appearances, you would think they are Christians. He explains that you can tell which ones are fake by observing their personal lives, using this as an example: "every good tree bears good fruit, but a bad tree bears bad fruit." If you find out that they are living a lifestyle of stealing, lying, going to bed with other people, and doing all types of evil, then they are not living like Christ. Avoid them.

He goes on to say that the person who does His teaching is truly His, and that the "many" fake Christians will be surprised when He sends them to hell.

Lucas, if you travel the narrow, hard-pressed road and obey the teachings of Jesus, you will have eternal life.

Blessings. Have a great day.

Day Fifteen

Matthew 8:1–17

Hello Lucas,

Jesus came to bring people the words of God, forgive their sins, and heal their bodies, minds, and emotions. He came to free them from the power of the devil. Here, we see Him doing that. Matthew reminds us that about seven hundred years earlier, God had foretold through the prophet Isaiah that His Son would come and do these exact things. "Surely he took up our pain and bore our suffering, yet we considered him punished by God, stricken by him, and afflicted. But he was pierced for our transgressions, he was crushed for our iniquities; the punishment that brought us peace was on him, and by his wounds we are healed" (Isaiah 53:4–5).

God is still doing these things today, and He will do them for you too. We have prayed for many blind, deaf, and sick people and seen them healed by the power of Jesus's name.

Here's a YouTube video link showing some of what we have experienced:

https://youtu.be/1nn0syt8O30

Blessings. Have a great day.

Day Sixteen

Matthew 8:18–34

Hello Lucas,

Large crowds were following Jesus. Occasionally someone would approach Him, offering to follow Him and become a full-time disciple. They might have been sincerely touched by something He taught, or they may have been attracted by the hope of popularity, power, and position that came with being associated with the Son of God. Nevertheless, Jesus was always upfront with them. Here you see Jesus addressing two of these would-be disciples. Both are distracted with other things and not "sold out" in their commitment, so Jesus shows them where their true affections lie.

It's the same today. People often come to God on their terms, not His. They want Him as their Savior but not as their Lord. They want salvation without a commitment. They want freedom but do not want to pay the price for it. If they approached any other relationship in such an uncommitted way, it would produce certain failure.

Throughout His teachings, Jesus is very clear in telling you that if you are going to follow Him, you must count the cost. "Those of you who do not give up everything you have cannot be my disciples" (Luke 14:33).

Lucas, never forget, salvation is free, but it will cost you everything that you have.

Blessings. Have a great day.

Day Seventeen

Matthew 9:1–17

Hello Lucas,

There were five types of Jewish religious and political leaders in Jesus's day:

1. Priests (Officiated sacrifices and offerings at the temple)
2. Pharisees (Taught the law of Moses)
3. Sadducees (Taught the law of Moses)
4. Scribes (Taught the law of Moses, preserved and made perfect copies of the holy scriptures)
5. Sanhedrin (Judicial council made up of elites, elders, Pharisees, Sadducees, and high-priest family)

These leaders followed strict religious traditions and knew scripture, but they did not know or love God. They controlled and manipulated the people for their own power and financial gain. Jesus knew this and always challenged their hypocrisy. They followed Him around, trying to trap Him in words so that they could have a reason to crucify Him.

It's possible to have religion but not truly know God. You must always love God deeply and not just blindly follow the church traditions or man-made rules.

Blessings. Have a great day.

Day Eighteen

Matthew 9:18–38

Hello Lucas,

Here, many people are receiving healing from Jesus because they believe and expect. They not only believe that God has the power but that He is willing to help them personally. Having faith is like having money from heaven, if you have it, things will happen. God is not only pleased when you have faith in Him, He wants you to believe Him for great things. Notice how Jesus is always trying to get people to "up their belief game" and how He responds when it comes to believing for miracles:

Verse 2:   "When Jesus saw their faith."
Verse 18:   "Put your hand on her, and she will live."
Verse 22:   "Jesus . . . said, 'your faith has healed you.' "
Verse 28:   " 'Do you believe that I am able to do this?' 'Yes, Lord,' they replied."
Verse 29:   "According to your faith let it be done to you."

The chapter ends with Jesus being moved deeply with compassion as He saw all the needs of the people. Many were sick and had diseases. They were harassed by evil spirits and needed a spiritual shepherd to help them. Jesus plainly responded that the workers were few and to ask God to send workers into the field.

Today that same worldwide spiritual need is still there. If you are willing to have faith and believe God, He is willing to do great things through you. As you go about your daily life, you could be one of the workers that Jesus longed to see. If you believe, all things are possible.

Blessings. Have a great day.

Day Nineteen

Matthew 10:1–13

Hello Lucas,

Jesus chose twelve of His disciples to be close to Him and follow Him during His three years of ministry. They were to be witnesses to all that He said and did as well as to His death and resurrection. He was training and empowering them to do ministry like He did. They were to start locally among the Jews first and then go through the whole world after His resurrection. Here, Jesus is teaching them how to deal with things as they go.

The one who accepts and follows Jesus is called His disciple. That word means "student," because you are to learn and do all that He taught. Tomorrow we will look at what He taught about sharing the Gospel in our world.

Blessings. Have a great day.

Day Twenty

Matthew 10:14–42

Hello Lucas,

There are some people who will never know God unless you introduce them to Him. If it were not for you, they would otherwise spend eternity in hell. As you share the good news, some people will accept it; some will reject it and hate you.

Jesus knew this, so He is explaining ahead of time what those who reject it may do:

1. Some will not welcome you.
2. You may be beaten.
3. You may be accused and taken to court.
4. Some of your family and friends will reject and betray you.
5. Others will persecute and hate you.

There is a principle in the kingdom of heaven called "redemptive suffering." It means that someone is willing to go through difficult times and suffer in order to bring help to someone else. It's like a firefighter who encounters a hazard while saving someone from a burning house. When anyone does that, they are considered a hero. Jesus purchased your salvation through the things which he suffered. Every lost soul is valuable to God and worth the price of suffering to save them. As you live out that attitude and lifestyle do not be afraid. If God cares for the simple birds, He is watching over every hair on your head. The one who suffers for Him has a very big reward in heaven.

Blessings. Have a great day.

Day Twenty-One

Matthew 11:1–18

Hello Lucas,

John the Baptist has been put in prison and will be beheaded for preaching the Gospel to King Herod. Herod had stolen his own brother's wife, and John told him that God did not approve.

Now that John was in prison and facing certain death, he was beginning to question the things that God had told him. He sent some of his followers to confirm that Jesus was the Savior from God.

Sometimes when you suffer for God, you may begin to doubt your faith and be tempted to give up. Jesus comforts John by calling him a great man in the kingdom of God. Then He does some miracles to prove to John's disciples that He is the Christ.

Jesus also encourages you not to be offended or fall away because of being identified as His follower. You should never be ashamed of Jesus. You should never be offended and fall away.

Blessings. Have a great day.

Day Twenty-Two

Matthew 11:19–30

Hello Lucas,

Jesus had traveled through many towns and villages ministering. Now, He takes time to evaluate their responses. He names several of the towns that did not repent, even though He brought the good news and performed great miracles there. Imagine the Son of God bringing the very words of God and doing the work of God in a town, and the people don't even respond. It's much like the saying, "The lights are on, but nobody's home." They are like a body that has no pulse; they are spiritually dead but unaware of it. He goes on to tell how that generation of residents will be held accountable on Judgment Day.

Since those places were unreceptive and proud, He makes an appeal to the people who are wearied by life's burdens, saying, "I will give you rest . . . my yoke is easy and my burden is light."

Lucas, it is not the proud, but the humble and burdened in heart that often respond to the kindness of God. Find those people in your town and generation and introduce them to God. If you do, they will thank you in a very big way on Judgment Day.

Blessings. Have a great day.

Day Twenty-Three

Matthew 12:1–37

Hello Lucas,

The religious leaders had created many traditions and rules that they required people to observe. The rules led people farther away from God. These leaders sent spies to follow Jesus and accuse Him of breaking their rules. Since Jesus came to show us the way to God, He told the truth and showed them where their teaching was wrong. He spoke very strongly against them because they were leading people to hell. He reminded them that everyone will give an account before God on Judgment Day.

There are still religious leaders today that teach their own rules and traditions. People blindly follow them into hell. It is important for you to know the truth that Jesus taught and obey Him. Then you will have confidence when you stand before God.

Blessings. Have a great day.

Day Twenty-Four

Matthew 12:38–50

Hello Lucas,

The religious leaders had the scriptures that described every detail about Jesus's coming, yet they asked Him to do a special sign to prove Himself. He had already performed many undeniable miracles, so Jesus said that the only sign He would show them was the one given by the prophet Jonah. Eight hundred years earlier, the prophet Jonah was three days in the belly of a fish and lived to tell about it. Likewise, Jesus would be placed in a tomb and come to life three days later. In saying this, He showed them that they should know and trust the Word of God.

At that time, Jesus's mother and brothers came to see Him. His mother, Mary, was blessed because she believed God and did His will. In verse 48, Jesus says an amazing thing! "Who is my mother, and who are my brothers? . . . Whoever does the will of my Father in heaven is my brother and sister and mother." Man-made traditions have given Mary an elevated status and intercessory role that God did not give her. Jesus brings clarity to this issue by placing Mary and every obedient Christian side by side, giving equal status to all who are obedient to God. You are nowhere instructed to pray to Mary. Instead, scripture says, "There is one God and one mediator between God and mankind, the man Christ Jesus, who gave himself as a ransom for all people" (1 Timothy 2:5–6).

If you continue to be obedient to God, you will be highly honored and favored by Him.

Blessings. Have a great day.

Day Twenty-Five

Matthew 13:1–17

Hello Lucas,

Jesus taught the crowds by using parables (picture stories that illustrate a lesson).

He taught that God sends His Word so that people will grow in Him. He said that there were four ways that people respond to His Word:

1. Some don't understand it, so they set it aside and lose it.
2. Some are happy to receive it, but when trouble comes, they give up.
3. Some receive it but are so busy with life, problems, and chasing money that there is no room for God.
4. Some receive, understand, and live it in a way that they grow and bring many others to God.

Notice only one out of four survived. Notice that all the seed (Word of God) that was planted was good seed. The problem was not with the seed; it was with the soil (the hearts of people).

You are God's garden. You must make sure that your ground is prepared and ready to receive God's Word. You want to be strong, healthy, and fruitful in your life and for the eternal kingdom of God.

Blessings. Have a great day.

Day Twenty-Six

Matthew 13:18–58

Hello Lucas,

Jesus continues to teach about the kingdom of God in parables. He shows that it's worth giving all that you have by comparing it to finding a hidden treasure or priceless jewels.

He puts people in two categories: those who are in the kingdom of God and those who are not. In verse 39, He explains that in the end, "the angels will come and separate the wicked from the righteous and throw [the wicked] into the blazing furnace."

In today's society, that is a not a politically correct message, but it is nevertheless true, and Jesus was not afraid to speak truth. You may tend to think the best of people and find it hard to think that someone could be evil. But God knows that the heart of every man is desperately wicked and needs to be reborn.

You have been born into God's kingdom, and He is at work changing your heart. It's important that you invite others to come into the kingdom of God also.

Blessings. Have a great day.

Day Twenty-Seven

Matthew 14:1–12

Hello Lucas,

John the Baptist preached against sin, called people to repent, baptized them in water, and pointed people to Jesus Christ the Son of God. Because of this, King Herod imprisoned John, and he eventually killed him.

Like Herod, many people love their lifestyle of sin so much that they either compromise or hate the truth. They do not want to hear it, and they will not receive it. When you tell them about God or speak the truth to them, they will try to make life miserable for you.

So then, why even waste your time on them? Because eventually some people you speak to will see and turn. When I was a senior in high school, I shared the Gospel with a lot of my classmates. Their responses varied. The class "tough guy" offered to meet me outside for a good old-fashioned "butt kicking," and two of the popular girls forever after referred to me as "Bible." It didn't seem to be received at the time, but now, fifty years later, all three of them are following Jesus and going to church. Those who completely reject you and God will be without excuse on Judgment Day. Your message to them will be evidence that God tried but they refused.

This life and suffering only lasts for a moment. Don't be discouraged. Because of your life and testimony, many will run up to you in heaven, thanking you for showing them the way to eternal life.

Blessings. Have a great day.

Day Twenty-Eight

Matthew 14:13–36

Hello Lucas,

Jesus used extreme events to teach His disciples to believe God for the impossible. He invited Peter to walk on water and showed the disciples how to feed five thousand families with a boy's lunch. Crowds were following Jesus. They were in a remote area and not able to buy food all day. He told his disciples to feed the crowd, but they could only find two fish and five loaves of bread. Jesus blessed it, and it multiplied as the disciples handed it out. Everyone ate a full meal, and there were leftovers.

In verse 31, Peter walked a short distance on the water and began to sink. Jesus helped him into the boat, and instead of congratulating him, Jesus asked, "Why did you doubt?" Jesus was teaching that all things are possible through God if you only believe and do not start doubting.

One time I needed around $450,000 to build a school in India. I only had a few dollars, but I told everyone about this Bible story. I believed that God could multiply and do the impossible. Because I believed, God did it! We started with empty pockets but completed and fully paid for the project.

God will do the same things for you. Only believe.

Blessings. Have a great day.

Day Twenty-Nine

Matthew 15:1–20

Hello Lucas,

Again, the religious leaders are challenging Jesus for not following their rules and traditions. He tells them plainly that their rules are man-made ideas and not from God. He tells them that they have rules that make them appear religious, but their hearts are far from God. It's like being married to but not in love with your spouse. You can have the title "husband" and live under the same roof but have no heart connection with your wife. The problem is always with the heart of man. Man-made rules and religion do not have the power to draw men to God or convert their souls. If you follow church rules only, it is like dancing without a partner.

You must always draw near to God with all your heart until you fall deeply in love with Him. If you dance with Him and follow His lead, He will continue to reveal Himself to you.

Blessings. Have a great day.

Day Thirty

Matthew 15:21–39

Hello Lucas,

A foreign woman came to Jesus requesting healing for her daughter. Jesus wanted to test her faith to see how serious she was, and to show others the importance of having faith. So He told her that He was called to minister to the Jews, and should He throw their food to the puppies? She replied that even the puppies get the scraps from the table. When Jesus heard her answer, He congratulated her in front of everyone by saying, "You have great faith! Your request is granted."

Many people get offended at God when He does not give them the answer they want, or He doesn't answer quick enough. Sometimes God is testing your faith. Sometimes He wants to give us something even better. Jesus never complained about people having too much faith. He always complimented people for having faith. He always challenged them to have more faith in God.

Continue to grow in faith, and God will do great things through you and for you.

Blessings. Have a great day.

Day Thirty-One

Matthew 16:1–20

Hello Lucas,

Jesus wanted to make sure His disciples understood that He was the Son of God. He also wanted them to know that He would suffer and die and rise from the dead three days later. So He asked them, "Who do people say the Son of Man is?" After they answered that question, He asked them, "Who do you say I am?"

Peter answered: "You are the Messiah, the Son of the living God."

Jesus told Peter that he was correct. He also said that the church would be built on that fact. Every building must have a foundation. Jesus did not say that Peter would be the foundation or that a pope would be the church's foundation. He said that the foundation would be this very fact: Jesus is the promised Christ, the Son of the living God.

Paul later referenced that truth when he said, "For no one can lay any foundation other than the one already laid, which is Jesus Christ" (1 Corinthians 3:11). Many religions will acknowledge that Jesus was a holy man or a prophet, but they will not admit that Jesus is the Christ, the Son of God.

The word *church* means "called out ones." Jesus has called you out of the world and helped you to believe that He truly is the Son of God. You are His church, His called out one, and you are built upon that foundational truth of who He is.

Blessings. Have a great day.

Day Thirty-Two

Matthew 16:21–28

Hello Lucas,

Jesus is telling His disciples that it is God's plan for Him to suffer, die, and resurrect on the third day.

In Isaiah chapter 53, scripture foretold that Jesus would first come as "Suffering Servant." Because of His obedience, God has made Him both King and Lord.

Peter does not understand this and is insisting that Jesus should be King first and not suffer. Jesus rebukes Peter, revealing that Peter's idea came directly from Satan.

Quite often, you may have your own ideas on how things in life should go and what God should do, but God has better plans.

As a Christian, you need to understand that Jesus is both King and Lord of your life. His ways and plans are best anyway.

Jesus replies, "Whoever wants to be my disciple must deny themselves and take up their cross and follow me. For whoever wants to save their life will lose it, but whoever loses their life for me will find it" (verses 24–25).

The cross is a symbol of death. You must die to your self-interest and live obedient to God's plans and ideas. If you allow Him to be King, then you are truly in the kingdom of God.

Blessings. Have a great day.

Day Thirty-Three

Matthew 17:1–13

Hello Lucas,

Jesus chose twelve disciples to witness all that He said and did. They saw Him live and fulfill the words that the prophets spoke about Him. They would see His death and resurrection. Now God wanted to tell them personally with His own voice that Jesus was the one He had sent. Jesus led three of His disciples up a mountain. God's presence came, and Jesus shone like the brightest light. Moses and the prophet Elijah appeared also. Then God spoke out loud, "This is my Son, whom I love; with him I am well pleased. Listen to Him!"

In order for a testimony to be valid in the judicial system, there must be ample witnesses. Here, God brought together Moses the law giver, Elijah the prophet, and Jesus's disciples, who all witnessed the voice and testimony of God concerning Jesus. Together, these men told the world what they saw and heard. Whoever rejects their account will stand defenseless before God. These eyewitnesses will testify against them, saying, "We told you, but you did not believe us."

Because of their testimony, you have heard and believed in Jesus. Let's pray that your friends' and families' eyes will be open to this shining truth as well.

Blessings. Have a great day.

Day Thirty-Four

Matthew 17:14–27

Hello Lucas,

Jesus's disciples try to cast a demon out of a boy. When they fail, Jesus arrives and casts it out. He tells them they failed because of their unbelief and small faith. He goes on to tell them that nothing will be impossible if they put their small faith to work, and that it's important to mix their prayer with it.

Here again, you see that God is always challenging the people to believe Him for great things.

To show this point, Jesus sends Peter to pay their taxes with empty hands. He tells Peter to catch a fish on his way and open its mouth. Inside, he finds a silver coin and pays the taxes.

When I was about eleven years old, my family was poor, and I was always asking God for help. At that time, we lived in a suburb of Las Vegas, Nevada. Outside of town, in the desert, I found a landfill dump that became my playground. One day I was playing there and found a pile of old clothes. It appeared that an old man had died, and his relatives scooped up his belongings and threw them away. As I dug through the pile, I found two small boxes. When I opened them up, I discovered a solid-gold, antique pocket watch and a gold ring with a pearl in it. I quickly returned home and gave the watch to my dad. To our surprise, it brought four months' wages when he sold it, more than enough to care for our needs. Because I was young and foolish, I gave the ring to a girl at school and never saw her again.

God wants to do powerful and unusual things in your life. You must allow your faith to grow and never underestimate God's ability. Your next big blessing may be found in something as simple as a little box or even a fish's mouth.

Blessings. Have a great day.

Day Thirty-Five

Matthew 18:1–14

Hello Lucas,

Several times, Jesus's disciples struggled with pride. Since Jesus had called and appointed them, they felt that they must be very important. They argued amongst themselves as to who would be the most important in God's kingdom. In this world, people are extremely competitive and will do almost anything to get ahead, including destroying others. Here, Jesus taught His disciples that the kingdom of heaven operates differently from the world and is not built by man's strength and pride.

Jesus brought a child forward and told them that childlike humility will get people ahead in His kingdom. He went on to point out the virtues of children and pronounce judgments against anyone who destroys a child's innocence. He continued that thought by saying it will be bad for the man who causes anyone to sin and then instructed His followers to cut off toxic relationships that cause them to sin.

Relationships are a powerful force that can bring either great blessings or heavy curses into the lives of others. You have joined a heavenly kingdom where humility in relationships is more honorable than arrogance and pride, and your holiness is more valuable than holding on to impure, toxic friendships. God wants you healed and whole in the way you relate to others, free from drama and dysfunction.

Blessings. Have a great day.

Day Thirty-Six

Matthew 18:15–35

Hello Lucas,

Jesus teaches how to deal with conflict.

What do you do when someone sins against you, especially when the person is a Christian?

Jesus gives two steps:

1. Deal with the person directly (verses 15–20).

You go to the person to discuss what they have done. If they will not listen, you bring witnesses and try again. If they reject you, you distance yourself from that relationship. The goal of this first step is to change their heart.

2. Deal with your heart attitude (verses 21–35).

You must not forget that God has forgiven your many sins, so extend that same kindness to others. The goal of this step is to keep your heart free from bitterness.

In 2016, I discovered that one of our India pastors was misappropriating many thousands of dollars from our ministry funds. This was a man whom I loved and had generously cared for since 2002. I dealt with him as Jesus instructed. When I did, he did much evil to me. It was hard, but God helped me to truly forgive him from my heart. I can no longer work with him, because so far, his heart has not changed. But I can honestly say that I do not want him to suffer judgment for anything that he has done against me.

Blessings. Have a great day.

Day Thirty-Seven

Matthew 19:1–12

Hello Lucas,

The religious leaders did not take their marriages seriously, so they tried to trap Jesus with a question about divorce. He took this opportunity to teach them how highly God values marriage by saying:

1. God created the male-female system, which by design means each one needs the other.
2. God created marriage. When the two exchange vows, God has officially "joined together" the couple into one inseparable unit.
3. The two are now one in soul and body, and from the two comes one flesh (a child). And since those who are joined to the Lord are one Spirit, they are one in spirit also.
4. Other relationships take second place to your spouse.
5. You should work through every problem and not divorce unless your spouse is sleeping around with others.

In our present society, many people live and sleep together in sin without committing to God's design. They do this because they do not understand the value and requirements that God places on marriage. So Jesus took time to carefully explain and help us understand.

Here's how it applies to your life:

1. If you are married and your wife is okay with you being a Christian, and if she is not sleeping around, remain married.
2. If you are living in an intimate, uncommitted relationship, you must resolve this issue with God now. Determine whether God wants you to marry or separate, but by all means, do not continue living in the sin of sexual immorality.
3. If you are single and looking for a wife, don't do the "continuous single dating" scene, and don't settle for the wrong person. Seek God and let Him bring a godly wife to you. He is preparing the person that is right for you.

Blessings. Have a great day.

Day Thirty-Eight

Matthew 19:13–30

Hello Lucas,

The disciples considered children to be unimportant and didn't want them bothering Jesus. But Jesus affirmed the children's value by blessing them and saying that the kingdom of heaven belongs to them.

In verse 16, a rich young man came to Jesus asking for eternal life. The man said that he had kept the commandments since childhood. Jesus helped him understand his heart's true condition by asking him to leave his riches and become his disciple. But the man sadly left. He did not realize that he loved his money more than he loved God. Jesus identified the love of money as a serious problem. Then He told His disciples they would get blessed "a hundred times as much" here on earth and have eternal life in heaven, because they had left all to follow Him.

Lucas, Jesus has called you directly to be His modern-day disciple! He will be faithful to show you what to give up and what remains the same. And if you faithfully obey Him, He will reward your obedience far more than you can imagine.

Blessings. Have a great day.

Day Thirty-Nine

Matthew 20:1–16

Hello Lucas,

Wherever Jesus went, He taught about the kingdom of heaven. Here, He tells a parable to show how generous God is with His kingdom:

1. God is described as the landowner.
2. Christians are described as day laborers.
3. Eternal life is described as wages paid at the end of the day.

In the story, the workers who worked all day were paid the same as the ones who worked only the last hour. Those who worked the whole day complained because the part-time help received full-time pay. Then God, the landowner, replied, "Are you envious because I am generous?"

I accepted Jesus when I was a young boy. I know someone who just accepted Jesus at age eighty-two. I have been working in the kingdom of God most of my life, and she has only been working a few years. But in the end, because of God's generosity, both of us will receive eternal life.

To those who have been in the kingdom a long time, it may not seem fair that a sinner can enter right before they die. But for the aged sinner destined for hell, he rejoices because of the generosity of God. You should rejoice too.

Blessings. Have a great day.

Day Forty

Matthew 20:17–34

Hello Lucas,

Jesus regularly tried to prepare His disciples for His coming death and resurrection, this time by telling them bluntly what was going to happen.

About this time, two of the disciples had their mother ask Jesus to appoint them to the highest places of honor in the kingdom of heaven. This problem of pride was an ongoing issue within the lives of the disciples. Jesus knew that and took this opportunity to teach them about humility and servanthood.

The kingdom of heaven is upside-down from the world system. In the world, the man who rules over many is honored. In the kingdom of God, the man who serves the best is honored. If you "climb the ladder of success," a lot of people get stepped on, and life becomes all about you. But when you become a humble servant, others are lifted up as you care for their eternal well-being. Jesus explained that even though He was the Son of God, He humbly became a servant so that others could be saved.

If Jesus humbled Himself for such a noble cause, you should adopt that same attitude. Be humble as you serve your family, your community, your workplace, and as you serve in the Lord's work. If you struggle like the disciples did, Jesus will keep working with you until you catch the idea.

Blessings. Have a great day.

Day Forty-One

Matthew 21:1–17

Hello Lucas,

Matthew begins to describe the last week of Jesus's work on earth. On Sunday, as prophesied, He rides a young donkey into Jerusalem. A large crowd follows Him, rejoicing and shouting loudly that He is God's Messiah. They want Him to take the throne from the Romans and lead as the Savior of the Jews and ruler of the world. It seems that all the people are for Him. Only five days later, the whole crowd will become disappointed and forsake Him. They do not understand that He must first come as suffering Savior for the sins of the world. Then when He returns the second time, He will come as ruling King of the world.

For now, Jesus leads the celebrating crowd to the temple and turns all the shop tables over, declaring that God's house is a house of prayer, not a den of robbers.

Sometimes God's plans will not make sense to you, but in the end it will all work out perfectly. Don't become discouraged and forsake Him like the crowds did. Wait things out and see the amazing outcome that He has planned.

Blessings. Have a great day.

Day Forty-Two

Matthew 21:18–46

Hello Lucas,

Jesus again taught His disciples the importance of having faith, telling them that nothing will be impossible if they believe. When He entered the temple, the religious leaders challenged His authority, so He dealt with their hypocrisy. He told them that God had appointed them to care for the people and lead them to God. Instead, they went their own way and were leading people into sin. He said that God sent John the Baptist to show them the way of righteousness, but they rejected Him. He told them that terrible sinners who believed and repented were entering the kingdom and were producing righteous fruit. Since the religious leaders rejected Jesus and produced no righteous fruit, they would be cast out.

When Jesus returns, He is expecting to find fruitful followers, not just religious-looking people. When you come to Jesus, you should begin to live a righteous life. You should be leading others to Jesus and helping them become righteous also.

One time I went into an Iowa cornfield and counted the number of kernels on a single ear of corn. There were around nine hundred. If God made one seed of corn to produce that many, God can help you lead nine hundred to Jesus in your lifetime too. You can live a life nine hundred times more fruitful and righteous than before.

Blessings. Have a great day.

Day Forty-Three

Matthew 22:1–22

Hello Lucas,

Jesus remains in the temple, teaching the large crowd. In just three days, the religious leaders will crucify Him, so He turns His attention to them. He tells them a parable that focuses on their lost spiritual condition. In it, He describes how they have rejected God and killed His Son and servants. He clearly tells them that God will destroy them.

Because they hate the truth, the religious leaders try to trap Jesus in His words so they can justify killing Him. They try trapping Him with a question on taxes, hoping to get Him condemned for treason. But God gives Him an answer that leaves them speechless.

Sometimes people say, "If God does this or that, I will believe in Him" or "If God appears to me, then I will believe in Him." Even though God appeared to the religious leaders, they did not recognize Him. Why? Because they loved their power and position more. Jesus told them that God would go everywhere, even the slums and ghettos, to find people who would sincerely love Him.

Blessings. Have a great day.

Day Forty-Four

Matthew 22:23–46

Hello Lucas,

The religious leaders continue asking Jesus questions, but they do not want answers, they are still trying to trap Him. He patiently gives them the answers and shows them where they went wrong by saying, "You are in error because you do not know the Scriptures or the power of God." Then He shows them the deeper root of their problem by saying that all of God's words and laws are based on loving God and loving others. In saying this, He shows them that they love themselves more than God.

Lucas, as a follower of Jesus, you must

1. study and know the scriptures so that you are not led astray;
2. understand that God's unlimited power is at work in and around you;
3. focus on loving God with all of your heart, soul, and mind, and loving others as much as you love yourself.

If you do these things, you will continue to grow in a productive relationship with God and others.

Blessings. Have a great day.

Day Forty-Five

Matthew 23:1–13

Hello Lucas,

Jesus spends this entire chapter openly rebuking and condemning the religious leaders. He lists their sins and hypocrisies and warns the crowd not to follow their ways. Jesus has never treated anyone else this harshly. Why? He tells us in verse 13, "You shut the door of the kingdom of heaven in people's faces. . . . Nor will you let those enter who are trying to."

A few years ago, a flock of geese were flying in a heavy rainstorm (monsoon). The lead bird decided to rest in a pond of water below, so he dove quickly. The rest of the birds followed him to their death. For the pond to which they were being led was not a pond at all. It was a water-soaked, hard-surface parking lot. All of them died upon impact.

Later, Jesus calls the religious leaders "blind guides." He shows them the root of their problem: "You clean the outside of the cup and dish, but inside they are full of greed and self-indulgence."

Lucas, keep a clean heart before the Lord. "Watch your life and doctrine closely. Persevere in them, because if you do, you will save both yourself and your hearers" (1 Timothy 4:16). Then you will be able to properly lead others into the kingdom of God.

Blessings. Have a great day.

Day Forty-Six

Matthew 23:14-39

Hello Lucas.

Over the past ten years, I have noticed that every year, at least two well-known Christian leaders are caught living extended sinful lifestyles. When that happens, the media celebrates by publishing every filthy detail, and delights in publicly denouncing Christians as "religious hypocrites." The confusion and shame that follow is unbearable, and many believers become disillusioned and fall away. Generally, the leader, when caught, lies, then makes light of it, and then ultimately says he's okay, because it's all covered by God's grace. They do all of that without ever admitting they were morally wrong or humbly repenting of their sin. And most often, they never express concern for their victims, who were devastated along the way.

This should not surprise us, because two thousand years ago, Jesus dealt with the very same behavior in the religious leaders of his day. Jesus openly exposed the many sins they were hiding in their hearts, so they could have an opportunity to repent and turn back to God. Let's look at the list:

1. They put heavy, religious loads on people.
2. They put on a religious show to get the people's acknowledgement and praise.
3. They loved to have positions of honor and distinguished titles.
4. They kept people from entering God's kingdom and persecuted people who were honestly trying.
5. They taught their own ideas and traditions and rejected God's Word.
6. They appeared to be clean but were filthy inside with greed and self-indulgence.
7. They appeared to be alive but were spiritually dead.
8. They thought they were okay, even though they were planning on killing Him and other Christians.

It appears that corrupt religious leaders feel confident because of their position and appointment from God. They feel secure no matter how depraved they become. These men can claim that their lifestyle "is all okay because of God's grace." But Jesus already gave the final word: "How will you escape being condemned to hell?"

Lucas, give diligence to your own heart, and if you ever encounter leaders like this, have nothing to do with them. Run the other way.

Blessings. Have a great day.

Day Forty-Seven

Matthew 24:1–8

Hello Lucas,

As Jesus left the temple with His disciples, they called His attention to its impressive beauty. King Herod had expanded the temple into a magnificent thirty-six-acre complex, (fourteen hectares). Jesus told them that this imposing structure would be demolished (and exactly thirty-seven years later, Emperor Titus destroyed it). Jesus took this opportunity to tell His disciples about other end-time catastrophes and events that would take place before His second return.

He said that the terrifying events would come like childbirth. When a woman begins delivery, her first contractions are small, with large gaps of relief in between. As the child comes closer, her pain increases, with shorter spaces between them. Finally, the contractions are continuous and the pain spikes permanently. Then the child comes.

Likewise, these difficult end-time events will increase in frequency and intensity. Then Jesus will come.

He is explaining this so that you will be prepared and not confused or tricked.

Blessings. Have a great day.

Day Forty-Eight

Matthew 24:9–35

Hello Lucas,

Have you ever wondered what the end of the world will be like? Jesus lists in order the events that will take place before He returns:

1. International wars are waged.
2. Famines and earthquakes occur.
3. All nations hate and kill Christians.
4. Many Christians give up their faith.
5. False prophets and false Christs come.
6. People become wicked and lose their love.
7. The Gospel is preached to all nations.
8. A world leader puts his own image in the temple in Jerusalem, demanding to be worshipped.
9. Armies invade and persecute Israel.
10. The sun and moon go dark.
11. Stars fall from the sky.
12. Jesus returns and brings to life His believers. Then He rules on earth for one thousand years.

Some of these things, like wars, have happened before. But remember, Jesus said that these will increase in severity and frequency until unbearable destruction covers the whole earth.

Lucas, Jesus left these words to encourage you, "I have told you these things, so that in me you may have peace. In this world you will have trouble. But take heart! I have overcome the world" (John 16:33).

Do not be shaken or afraid, because Jesus has warned you ahead. You have a bright future with Him.

Blessings. Have a great day.

Day Forty-Nine

Matthew 24:36–51

Hello Lucas,

In three days, Jesus will be crucified, and three days later He will raise to life, then ascend to heaven. Soon He will return as righteous King of all the Earth.

In verse 36, Jesus warns His followers to be ready and prepared for His return, so that they are not caught off guard.

He reminds them how the unprepared, sinful world was destroyed by Noah's flood.

He has already told you the events that will happen before His return, and He tells you the exact generation. Later you are told the "times" and "seasons." But Jesus warns you, "Only the Father" knows the actual "day or hour."

He tells a parable about a Christian worker who thought that Jesus was taking a long time returning, so the worker thought he could enjoy the pleasures of sin without being caught. That Christian was surprised when Jesus returned suddenly and threw him into hell with the other sinners.

Jesus wants you to be spiritually awake and prepared for His return. He loves you, so He has warned ahead of time.

Blessings. Have a great day.

Day Fifty

Matthew 25:1–30

Hello Lucas,

Jesus is using parables to explain how things will go for His followers when He returns. Let's look closer:

The Parable of the Ten Virgins

1. The ten virgins are people who identify as Christians awaiting their groom's arrival.
2. The coming Bridegroom is Jesus.
3. The lamp o l is the indwelling presence and work of the Holy Spirit.
4. The five foolish virgins are Christians in name only who looked religious outwardly. But they had never allowed the Holy Spirit to fill or transform their lives. They were unprepared and were shut out of heaven.
5. The five wise virgins had welcomed the presence of the Holy Spirit and His work within them and on a moment's notice, radiated it. They were prepared and welcomed into the wedding banquet.

In verse 14, the "Parable of the Bags of Gold" (also called "Parable of the Talents") explains that every Christian has been given resources by God, and He expects us to show an increase when Jesus returns. In this story the faithful ones were given positions of honor and responsibility in heaven, but the unfaithful were cast into hell.

Imagine receiving free forgiveness from sins but not producing a life of righteousness.

Imagine being saved from hell fire, but then passively watching as the other victims perish. The kingdom of heaven is like that. When Jesus returns, you do not want to stand before Him unchanged and empty-handed.

Lucas, God has given you everything needed to live a fruitful, changed life. He has given you resources and abilities to bring dying souls into His kingdom. If you are obedient in these small things now, He will make you a faithful steward over much more in heaven.

Blessings. Have a great day.

Day Fifty-One

Matthew 25:31–46

Hello Lucas,

In verse 31, Jesus tells how He will separate the righteous from the wicked when He returns. The righteous will receive eternal life in the kingdom of heaven, and the wicked will receive eternal punishment in hell.

He credits the righteous people for taking care of His needs, and He condemns the wicked for refusing to help Him.

Both groups are confused and ask when they saw Him with these needs.

Jesus replies, "Whatever you did for one of the least of these brothers and sisters of mine, you did for me."

Earlier, Jesus said that we are His brothers. When you care for fellow Christians in need, Jesus considers it a personal favor toward Him. The world will recognize that you are a genuine Christian because of the love that you show toward others. And Jesus will recognize you as one of the righteous among the nations. Lucas, continue to do good to all and walk in love toward your brothers in Christ.

Blessings. Have a great day.

Day Fifty-Two

Matthew 26:1–13

Hello Lucas,

In a couple of days, Jesus will be crucified. His death is centered around a Jewish festival called Passover. It celebrates the time when God delivered the Jews from slavery and poured out His wrath against their Egyptian oppressors. The Jews were instructed to slay a lamb and put its blood over the door and windows of their homes. When the death angel saw the blood, he would "pass over" without harming them. Remember earlier when John baptized Jesus? You'll read later in the book of John that before he baptized Jesus, John announced, "Look, the Lamb of God, who takes away the sin of the world!" (John 1:29). Passover is what John was talking about. It was God's plan to offer His Son as your Passover lamb during the Passover festival, His blood to wash away your sins.

In verse 6, a woman comes with a burial perfume and anoints Jesus. The perfume costs a whole year's wages and is made from flowers that only grow in the Himalayas, three thousand miles away from her home. Jesus acknowledges it as an act of kindness done in preparation for His coming death. Imagine Jesus smelling like beautiful perfume while being beaten and crucified for your sins.

By faith you have applied Jesus's blood to your heart, and when God sees that, His wrath will pass over you. Now God has also brought you out of slavery. God has poured out these blessings like sweet smelling perfume upon your life. Enjoy the forgiveness and freedom!

Blessings. Have a great day.

Day Fifty-Three

Matthew 26:14–75

Hello Lucas,

The Passover celebration begins. The main event is the evening meal, which Jesus shares with His disciples. It is called "The Last Supper" because He will be crucified the next day. During the meal, Jesus announces that a "New Covenant" will be established through the breaking of His flesh, and the shedding of His blood.

What is this "New Covenant" that Jesus mentions? The old covenant (the Ten Commandments and the law) was given through Moses. But God had promised a new and better one.

" 'This is the [new] covenant I will make . . . declares the Lord. 'I will put my law in their minds and write it on their hearts. I will be their God, and they will be my people. . . . I will forgive their wickedness and will remember their sins no more' " (Jeremiah 31:3–34). Praise God! Because of Jesus, your Passover Lamb, this New Covenant agreement belongs to you!

Around midnight, Jesus led His disciples to a private garden to pray and ask the Father for strength to endure the crucifixion. As a man, He did not want to suffer. He could have called down twelve thousand angels to save Him; instead He was obedient to God's plan even unto death.

Around 4 a.m., Judas the betrayer led the religious leaders to Jesus's hidden prayer spot. When they arrested Him, all of His disciples fled. His enemies finally had their way with Him. They quickly held a mock trial and convicted Him of blasphemy for admitting to being the Son of God.

Peter and John watched the proceeding from a distance. When someone recognized Peter, he denied even knowing Jesus. Five hundred years earlier, Zechariah the prophet foretold, "Strike the shepherd, and the sheep will be scattered" (Zechariah 13:7). Jesus would have to face suffering alone.

Blessings. Have a great day.

Day Fifty-Four

Matthew 27:1–26

Hello Lucas,

The religious leaders unjustly condemned Jesus to death. They needed approval to execute Him, so they brought Jesus before Pilate, the Roman governor. After hearing the testimony, Pilate declared Him to be innocent. The religious leaders stirred up the crowd, putting pressure on Pilate until he gave in. He washed his hands of the affair and turned Jesus over to be crucified. Jesus was innocent and should have been released, but God was using the situation to accomplish His plan. Once Judas realized the outcome of his betrayal, he hung himself and died.

Scripture tells us that Jesus was chosen before the creation of the world but was revealed in these last times (Revelation 13:8). God knew that man would sin, so before He created the world, He made a plan to save us. He hid that plan so that Satan could not disturb it.

God gave over three hundred prophecies detailing the plan. When looked at separately, no one could understand, but His mystery of salvation unfolded clearly as Jesus's life fulfilled each prophecy. It was much like a puzzle. Each piece is distinct, and you don't get the picture until they all fit together.

Blessings. Have a great day.

Day Fifty-Five

Matthew 27:27–66

Hello Lucas,

Before creation, Jesus was destined to suffer, die, and resurrect for your sins. Eight hundred years earlier, the prophet Isaiah, in chapter 53, foretold that Jesus would experience these things:

1. Be denied justice
2. Be beaten beyond recognition
3. Collapse carrying the cross
4. Be stripped naked and humiliated
5. Be hung on the cross with nails
6. Be despised and mocked by onlookers
7. Be alone from God while sacrificed
8. Be pierced with a spear
9. Make his grave with the wicked, and with the rich in his death
10. See the light of life and be satisfied

And that is exactly what happened. Jesus was condemned and crucified along with two wicked thieves and buried in a rich man's tomb. The religious leaders remembered that Jesus said He would raise to life on the third day. So they put a seal on the tomb and requested soldiers from Pilate to guard it.

We find in the Gospel of John that Jesus said earlier, "Unless a kernel of wheat falls to the ground and dies, it remains only a single seed. But if it dies, it produces many seeds" (John 12:24). Jesus had to die for your sins, be buried in the ground, and raise to life in order to bring forth many sons. Neither Satan nor the religious leaders understood that.

Lucas, as a follower of Jesus, you understand that you too must die to your old nature, your old way of living, in order to bring forth the fruit of righteousness.

Blessings. Have a great day.

Day Fifty-Six

Matthew 28:1–10

Hello Lucas,

Jesus was placed in the tomb on Friday night and raised to life Sunday morning. What happened while His body lay there? Scripture tells us that Jesus descended into hell, disarmed Satan, preached to the disobedient, and brought captive souls back from the abyss. "I am the Living One; I was dead, and now look, I am alive for ever and ever! And I hold the keys of death and Hades" (Revelation 1:18).

After Jesus defeated Satan, God sent the Holy Spirit to raise Jesus's body to life, and He sent angels to roll the tombstone back. When the guards saw this, they went into shock and became like dead men. Some of the women who were His disciples came and saw Jesus resurrected. He sent them ahead to tell the others that He was alive.

Now that you belong to Jesus, you no longer need to be afraid. He holds the keys and has delivered you from the power of death and hell. When He returns, He will resurrect you to eternal life.

Blessings. Have a great day.

Day Fifty-Seven

Matthew 28:11–20

Hello Lucas,

Earlier, the religious leaders asked Jesus to prove that He was God's Son, so He told them that He would die and resurrect to life on the third day. After Jesus's resurrection, the guards told the leaders everything that had happened at Jesus's tomb. Instead of accepting the truth, they bribed the guards to change their story. Some people will never accept Jesus, or the truth, even if He came to them. It shows that they love sin more than God.

By obeying God's plan, Jesus conquered death, hell, and the grave. So God gave Him all authority and power in heaven and earth. Jesus gave that authority to His followers and commanded them to go into the entire world and do this:

1. Make disciples who believe in Jesus.
2. Baptize (submerse in water) in the name of the Father, Son, and Holy Spirit.
3. Teach others to obey everything Jesus commanded.

About fifty-five million people die each year. Jesus has entrusted their spiritual well-being to you. You must take His power and authority into the world and reach as many as possible.

Blessings. Have a great day.

CHAPTER THREE

Mark

Day Fifty-Eight

Mark 1:1–13

Hello Lucas,

Throughout history, God spoke to the world through His prophets, one of which was Malachi. Then for four hundred years, He became silent. Mark begins his gospel by taking us back to those last words of God. "I will send my messenger, who will prepare the way before me. Then suddenly the Lord you are seeking will come to his temple" (Malachi 3:1). Approximately one hundred years before Malachi, Isaiah prophesied of the same thing: "A voice of one calling: In the wilderness prepare the way for the LORD; make straight in the desert a highway for our God" (Isaiah 40:3). When someone says the same thing twice and then becomes silent, we should consider their last words.

Mark is showing us that John the Baptist was that messenger prophesied about, who prepared the people's hearts to receive the promised Christ. He baptized Jesus and testified that Jesus was the Son of God. After four hundred years, the prophecy was fulfilled. God broke His silence and spoke to us directly through His promised Son.

In verse 12, Jesus was led to the desert to be tempted by Satan. Even though He was tempted in every way like us, He did not sin. God appointed Jesus to be your High Priest, and He can effectively sympathize with your temptations and weakness. Regarding this topic, God tells us, "Let us then approach God's throne of grace with confidence, so that we may receive mercy and find grace to help us in our time of need" (Hebrews 4:16).

Lucas, Jesus knows all of your temptations. Never be ashamed to bring those issues to God's throne of grace. Jesus is already there, compassionately explaining your situation to your heavenly Father.

Blessings. Have a great day.

Day Fifty-Nine

Mark 1:14–45

Hello Lucas,

Jesus starts His public ministry by telling people to repent (turn from their sins), just like John the Baptist had taught. Repentance from sin and belief in Jesus is the central truth of the Gospel (good news) message. You were an enemy and separated from God because of your evil behavior. In order to enter the kingdom of God, you had to put down your weapons (repent) and trust Jesus to wash your sins away. This was the good news that Jesus taught.

Seven hundred years earlier, God had promised through the prophet Isaiah that Jesus would come and preach good news to the poor, heal the sick, cast out devils, and comfort the sad. "The Spirit of the Sovereign Lord is upon me, because the Lord has anointed me to proclaim good news to the poor. He has sent me to bind up the brokenhearted, to proclaim freedom for the captives and release from darkness for the prisoners, to proclaim the year of the Lord's favor" (Isaiah 61:1–2). Now we see Jesus doing that. He is choosing disciples to help Him as He goes from village to village preaching to the poor. He casts out many evil spirits and cures multitudes of sick people along the way.

Satan came into the world to kill, steal, and bring destruction into your life, but Jesus came to give you freedom and a new life overflowing with amazing things.

Blessings. Have a great day.

Day Sixty

Mark 2:1–12

Hello Lucas,

As Jesus went throughout the villages preaching and teaching, He healed and delivered people in these different ways:

1. Commanded evil spirits to go
2. Touched the sick
3. Said, "Be clean," to the diseased
4. Said, "Take your mat and walk," to the paralyzed

Sometimes it was Jesus's faith and compassion that caused the healing, and other times it was the person's own faith and belief. There were even times when the faith and actions of a friend brought about the needed results.

In today's passage, Jesus was in a house so crowded that a paralyzed man could not enter for healing. His friends carried him on a mat to the roof, made a hole, and lowered him to Jesus. Seeing their faith, He forgave the man his sins. The religious leaders challenged Jesus's authority to forgive sins. So He healed the man. This healing miracle proved His authority.

No Christian should have to walk alone. If you surround yourself with friends that have faith, you can carry each other in times of trouble. Together your faith will bring results from God.

Blessings. Have a great day.

Day Sixty-One

Mark 2:13–28

Hello Lucas,

Jesus calls Levi (also known as Matthew), a tax collector, to follow Him. Tax collectors were hated by the community because they worked for the oppressive Roman government and often cheated people out of money. Jesus had dinner at Levi's house along with other guests who were sinners. The religious leaders asked Jesus why He associated with people like this. He answered by saying that the sick need a doctor and that He came to call sinners.

Jesus explained why He chose sinners instead of religious leaders to be His disciples and build God's kingdom. "No one sews a patch of unshrunk cloth on an old garment. Otherwise, the new piece will pull away from the old, making the tear worse." The religious leaders were like old clothes, unwilling to receive the "new-life" truth from Jesus. But the sinners gladly received and repented.

Lucas, you must always be willing to set aside your ideas and traditions and receive the truth of God so that He can continue to change your heart and life as well.

Blessings. Have a great day.

Day Sixty-Two

Mark 3:1–6

Hello Lucas,

Imagine that your hand has been shriveled for many years. You cannot grab anything or even do simple daily tasks. You are tired of relying on others for daily survival. Then imagine that someone walks into the room who has the ability to heal you. In an instant, your life could be changed, and your problems would be solved, but someone who does not want you to be healed stands in the way.

That is exactly what happened. The religious and political leaders stood between Jesus and a crippled man. They had their plans, and they didn't want Jesus getting respect for healing the man. They did not care about who suffered as long as they accomplished their goals. This has always been the problem. Man's stubborn plans against God's plans. That is why Jesus said, "Whoever wants to be my disciple must deny themselves and take up their cross and follow me" (Matthew 16:24). Jesus prevailed and the crippled man was healed.

If you set aside your plans and agendas and let God live His life through you, many suffering people will be set free.

Blessings. Have a great day.

Day Sixty-Three

Mark 3:7–35

Hello Lucas,

Jesus was ministering so powerfully that large crowds from many cities followed Him. He appointed twelve of His disciples to help Him and gave them power to cast out devils and to do great miracles.

Because His fame spread so quickly, some did not understand. His family said, "He is out of his mind." The religious leaders said that He was doing things by the power of a great demon. Jesus told them that Satan cannot fight against himself, or he will fall. He explained that He was doing the work of God by the power of the Holy Spirit.

In verse 31, His family still did not understand and wanted to take Him away. Jesus paid no attention to their nonsense. Instead, He said, "Whoever does God's will is my brother and sister and mother."

When you pledge your life to God, others around you may no longer understand. You may be rejected by family members. But Jesus has called you His brother and promised that He will never leave or forsake you.

Blessings. Have a great day.

Day Sixty-Four

Mark 4:1–20

Hello Lucas,

As the large crowds followed Jesus, He taught them about the kingdom of heaven by telling them parables (stories). The people loved to hear His stories, but many did not understand their meaning. One of the goals of a teacher is to teach in a way so that the students can completely understand the subject. So why did Jesus use a method that left so many people in the dark?

In verses 9–12, He explained by saying, "Whoever has ears to hear, let them hear." Of course, everyone has ears, but not everyone is willing to receive the truth. He went on to explain that the kingdom secrets were given to Jesus's true followers and that the insincere crowds would see but not perceive, hear but not understand.

Here you find a very important principle: If you are hungry and sincere, God will teach you His secrets, otherwise you will remain ignorant about eternal life.

Lucas, continue to keep an open ear and open heart so that you can receive all that God has to teach you.

Blessings. Have a great day.

Day Sixty-Five

Mark 4:21–41

Hello Lucas,

Wouldn't it be interesting if you could soar past the clouds and stars and enter heaven for a day? You could ask all the questions that you want and see with your own eyes what the kingdom of heaven is like. God wants you to know these things too; that's why Jesus was always teaching about the kingdom of heaven. In verse 21, He said that God wants this truth to shine like a light for everyone to see.

Jesus explained that God's kingdom is full of life; everything and everyone within it is always b essed and growing. His kingdom started with only a single seed (Jesus giving His life), and it grew into a plant that has filled the whole world. In His kingdom, God gives to His people, they give to others, and then again God gives them even more. Everyone that receives the Word of God grows by day and night, and their life produces the fruit of righteousness.

The kingdom of God is a place of life, growth, and multiplication. That is why Jesus has taught you to pray, "Your kingdom come, your will be done, on earth as it is in heaven" (Matthew 6:10). All the beauty, justice, and blessing that abide within heaven is now making its residence here on earth and within you. It will radiate through your life as you yield yourself more and more to this glory of God.

Blessings. Have a great day.

Day Sixty-Six

Mark 5:1–20

Hello Lucas,

After teaching the crowds, Jesus and His disciples crossed the lake in a boat. A storm came and almost sank them, but Jesus spoke and calmed the storm. He challenged the disciples for not using their faith to do it. When they arrived at the shore, a crazy man full of demons met them. The demons spoke, saying, "My name is Legion, for we are many." With a simple command, Jesus cast the thousands of demons out and into nearby pigs. The herd of pigs ran into the lake and drowned.

The people of that area came and saw the man clothed and in his right mind, and they saw that all the pigs were dead. This powerful deliverance scared them, so they asked Jesus to leave. The freed man asked to go along, but Jesus said no: "Go home to your own people and tell them how much the Lord has done for you, and how he has had mercy on you." So he went throughout ten local cities telling everyone.

Imagine life spiraling out of control until you become mentally ill, homeless, naked, isolated, demon possessed, and uncontrollable. Then after encountering Jesus, you are left healed, loved, clothed, and in your right mind. All you want to do is be with the one who brought such healing to you. But instead, your deliverer sends you away to help others.

Like the crowds here, some people are not ready to receive Jesus and could possibly end up in hell. Even though they don't understand Him yet, He loves them so much that He sends you to help them. It is His hope that they may gladly listen to your story as you tell how God has changed your life.

Blessings. Have a great day.

Day Sixty-Seven

Mark 5:21–43

Hello Lucas,

The religious leaders always opposed Jesus, but then one of their daughters became deathly ill. The leader humbled himself and asked Jesus to go heal his daughter. On the way, they encountered opposition that could have caused the leader to lose his faith and miracle.

1. Crowds got between him and Jesus.
2. Other sick people stopped Jesus.
3. Some told the man that his daughter had died.
4. Some laughed at Jesus when they arrived.

Jesus helped the man stay focused and not lose his faith by saying, "Don't be afraid; just believe." Because of those words, the man received his daughter back to life.

Faith is believing in God's words and ability even when it doesn't make sense or when it seems impossible. If you continue to believe, you will receive. But if you lose your faith along the way, you will receive nothing. By faith you have received Jesus as God's Son. By faith you will believe in Him for many things. On the way, opposition from others will come. Jesus will always help you with the similar words: "Don't be afraid; just believe." If you hold on, you will receive.

Blessings. Have a great day.

Day Sixty-Eight

Mark 6:1–13

Hello Lucas,

After being welcomed all across the land of Israel, Jesus returned home and taught. His neighbors were amazed at His extreme wisdom and ability to do miracles. But instead of receiving His words and healing, they thought, *Jesus is only a local boy; what is special about Him?* Because of their unbelief, He couldn't accomplish much among them. Sometimes the hardest people to help spiritually are family members. They still view us as "little Johnny," who knows nothing. They cannot receive the goodness of God, because it is offered through us.

My wife and I tried for years to share the Gospel with her father. He would not receive it from us. So every day for five years, we privately prayed for him. Then on his deathbed, he listened to the same message from our friend and gladly accepted Jesus.

Lucas, go forward with sharing the Gospel with your family and friends as they allow you to do so. Pray for them by name daily. If you do this, God will use every resource to draw them, even if it is someone else.

Blessings. Have a great day.

Day Sixty-Nine

Mark 6:14–56

Hello Lucas,

Because of self-interest, King Herod had killed John the Baptist, putting an end to his ministry. As Jesus continued to minister and perform miracles, His fame spread, and all eyes were on Him. This fulfilled John's words: "He must become greater; I must become less" (John 3:30).

Do you remember that earlier Jesus had delivered a man from a legion of demons, and the people of that area were afraid and asked Jesus to leave? Now, when Jesus returned to that very place, and when the people recognized Him, they were happy. They brought all their sick and begged Him to touch and heal everyone. What made the difference? It was because the delivered man stayed behind and went through the area telling the people what Jesus had done for him.

There is power in your testimony. You may not know a lot about God, but you know what He has done in your life. And as you share your story, others who have been confused about or afraid of Jesus will now be drawn to Him.

Blessings. Have a great day.

Day Seventy

Mark 7:1–23

Hello Lucas,

The religious leaders had many cleansing rituals, ceremonies, and traditions that they observed. When they saw the disciples eating without washing their hands, they confronted Jesus about it. In turn, Jesus rebuked the leaders and said, "You have let go of the commands of God and are holding on to human traditions." He went on to explain that whatever comes from the heart makes a man unclean, not what goes in his mouth.

There is a certain comfort that comes from having religious traditions, but traditions do not have the power to transform your heart. If you only do these, you are like a man who puts on a clean suit but has never taken a bath. You will certainly look good outwardly, but your body will be dirty and stink.

If you follow the commands and Word of God instead of traditions, your heart will be clean. Then your outward actions will reflect it also.

Blessings. Have a great day.

Day Seventy-One

Mark 7:24–37

Hello Lucas,

For two years, Jesus had been going everywhere preaching the good news, healing the sick and delivering these possessed by evil spirits. In verses 31–35, He heals a deaf and mute man in a strange way. Jesus puts His fingers into the man's ears. He spits, then touches the man's tongue and says "Be opened." The man begins to hear and speak plainly.

In 2002, I was in Namphainong, India, near the Myanmar border, preaching. As I was finishing my message, someone brought a mute boy to be healed. I was young back then and became nervous as two thousand Hindus watched to see what would happen. God's inner voice told me to have the boy stick out his tongue and then slap it. I had to force myself to do such a crazy thing. But when I did and said, "In Jesus's name," the boy's tongue was loosed, and he spoke clearly. In Isaiah 55:9 God says, "As the heavens are higher than the earth, so are my ways higher than your ways and my thoughts than your thoughts."

Lucas, never limit God. Every spiritual thing doesn't need to make complete sense to your rational thinking. If you allow God to do things His "strange" way, you will always receive the results needed.

Blessings. Have a great day.

Day Seventy-Two

Mark 8:1–21

Hello Lucas,

Large crowds followed Jesus for three days and had no food. So for a second time, He miraculously fed thousands with just a handful of bread and fish. After eating, He and His disciples left. On the way, Jesus warned them to beware of the yeast of the religious leaders. The disciples thought He was correcting them because they didn't have enough bread. Jesus was surprised at their response and said, "Are your hearts hardened?" They had fed five thousand and had more leftovers than they started with. Then they understood that Jesus meant beware of the yeast (false teachings) of the religious leaders.

Jesus was trying to talk about spiritual things, but the disciples were thinking from an earthly viewpoint. So He identified their problem as "hard hearts."

Lucas, if you keep your spiritual antennae up and focus on spiritual things instead of having just an earthly point of view, your heart will stay sharp and not become hard. Then you will always understand what the Holy Spirit is saying to you.

Blessings. Have a great day.

Day Seventy-Three

Mark 8:22–38

Hello Lucas,

A blind man was brought to Jesus to be healed, but he only received partial sight. It wasn't until Jesus touched him the second time that his sight was fully restored. Jesus had all the power, but the man was not healed immediately. Why? Because the man's friends who brought him had some faith but not enough. However, when the blind man began to see a little, his own faith grew enough to receive complete healing.

Faith is believing in God and His ability for things that you cannot see yet. It's believing that every word that God has spoken is true. Faith is like everything else; you can have a lot or a little amount of it. It's like a muscle; if you use it it will get strong.

In the kingdom of God, you receive everything that you need through faith alone. God has told you in Romans 1:17, "From first to last, just as it is written: 'The righteous will live by faith.' " That's why Jesus was always challenging the people to grow in their faith and believe God.

Begin now to exercise your faith. Believe God for small things, and the big ones will quickly follow.

Blessings. Have a great day.

Day Seventy-Four

Mark 9:1–32

Hello Lucas,

Understanding the many prophesies about Jesus's coming is like opening a puzzle box. You must lay them out one by one and match the colors and shapes. Piece by piece the picture becomes clearer. Jesus led three of His disciples up a mountain to show them two more puzzle pieces:

1. God spoke to them from heaven, "This is my Son, whom I love."
2. Jesus explained that John the Baptist fulfilled the prophesies of Elijah coming ahead of Christ.

In verse 22, a father asked Jesus to cast a demon out of his son. Jesus said it was possible if the man believed. The man said, "I do believe; help me overcome my unbelief!" This man had small faith and asked Jesus to help him overcome his unbelief. That quick, Jesus answered the prayer and delivered the son.

Sometimes you will find that your belief in God's ability in a situation will get challenged as doubts creep in. You know that God does miracles for others but maybe feel that your need is not as important to Him.

I have often prayed, "God help my unbelief," and He has always answered my prayer. He will do the same for you.

Blessings. Have a great day.

Day Seventy-Five

Mark 9:33–50

Hello Lucas,

Jesus begins to teach His disciples how to properly work with others in God's kingdom.

1. It is not your great talent or leadership that accomplishes God's purposes.
2. He who serves others best accomplishes most.
3. No matter how small and childish your position looks, you are representing God and are respected because of it.
4. Don't obstruct others who are doing God's work just because they are not a part of your organization or methods.
5. If someone leads a believer into sin, they will be severely punished by God.
6. If a relationship leads you into sin, it's better to leave that relationship rather than end up in hell.
7. Everyone's relationship with God will be tested by fire to see if it is sincere.
8. Do your best to be at peace with each other.

Blessings. Have a great day.

Day Seventy-Six

Mark 10:1–12

Hello Lucas,

Whenever God plans to do something, He always backs it up with a legal contract. Throughout the Bible, He made and honored many covenants, promises, and agreements.

Terms of a contract express the desires, obligations, and benefits for both parties. Disputes are settled quickly when there is a written agreement. If someone forgets or violates the terms, both can go back and read the agreement. Circumstances can change, but both parties are assured that the terms they agreed to will be fulfilled.

The religious leaders questioned Jesus about whether it was okay to end a marriage covenant. He told them that it was a contract that God had established and that He expected them to honor it. He said if they did not honor it, it was because their hearts were hard, and they were sinning.

Lucas, once you enter into a marriage contract with your wife, remember that it is a covenant that God created. Honor it with all your heart.

Blessings. Have a great day.

Day Seventy-Seven

Mark 10:13–52

Hello Lucas,

Jesus continues teaching how the kingdom of heaven is different from the world:

1. You do not enter it by your own wisdom and strength but by simply receiving it like a little child would.
2. It's almost impossible to enter it if you are wealthy and mainly focused on money. However, He adds, "All things are possible with God."
3. If you give up things now or suffer loss for following Him, you will be rewarded both here and eternally.
4. Don't try to be the top dog, because the one who serves others best is greater.

If you consider closely Jesus's teachings on the kingdom, you will truly be a heavenly citizen.

In verse 47, a blind man was shouting for Jesus to heal him. The people were annoyed and tried to shut him up. But Jesus heard and healed the man.

Like this story, people may try to discourage you as you pursue Jesus, but if you do not give up, you will receive all that He has for you.

Blessings. Have a great day.

Day Seventy-Eight

Mark 11:1–19

Hello Lucas,

Jesus became popular with the general public because of His miracles and powerful teaching. Amazed, they said that He was like the great prophets of old. In this passage, they came together in a triumphal procession, shouting His praise and declaring that Jesus was the Messiah, King of the Jews. They cast their cloaks before Him, waving palm branches while ushering Him into Jerusalem.

Jesus was the Messiah, not because the people finally realized it but because God planned it and prophesied about all of these events ahead of time.

Arriving at Jerusalem, they entered the temple where Jesus fulfilled more prophesies. He threw out the market tables and declared that God's house is a place of prayer. The people were hoping that Jesus would now set up His kingdom and rule in Jerusalem. But that wasn't God's immediate plan.

God's plans may not always meet your expectations. But as you submit to His Word and His leadership, the outcome will always be best.

Blessings. Have a great day.

Day Seventy-Nine

Mark 11:20–33

Hello Lucas,

Peter points out that a tree Jesus had cursed earlier the day before had already withered. So Jesus uses the event to teach His disciples about faith and forgiveness. He tells them to have faith in God for impossible things and that if they keep believing, they will receive what they prayed for. He explains that doubt is the enemy of faith.

In verse 25, He explains that your heart must be free from bitterness and unforgiveness when you come in prayer to God. In another place, He instructs you to mend relationships with other Christians before taking your financial offerings to God.

In saying these things, Jesus is showing you that He wants you to grow in faith until miracles become a natural part of your life. He is also showing you that He wants you to grow in love for your brothers in Christ until healthy relationships become a natural part of your life.

Blessings. Have a great day.

Day Eighty

Mark 12:1–27

Hello Lucas,

Jesus told the religious leaders a parable that exposed their condition. God had made them leaders for the purpose of blessing people and producing godly fruit. Instead, they used their authority to sustain their sinful lifestyle and personal profit. He told how they had killed and abused the prophets who confronted them, and they would also kill Him, the Son of God. They asked many tricky questions, trying to trap Him. So He told them that God would destroy them and give the kingdom to other people who would be faithful.

Because they rejected Him and were going to kill Him, He told them that the prophets foretold that they would do that. "The stone the builders rejected has become the cornerstone; the LORD has done this, and it is marvelous in our eyes" (Psalm 118:22–23). Some people, even some Christian leaders only want to use God for their benefit. They want a Savior, but not a Lord. They want eternal life, but not a changed life. They want God to submit to their prayers, but they don't want to obey Him.

Because of Jesus, God has given His kingdom to you. He wants you to love Him and produce a righteous, fruitful life. You must never use this as an opportunity for self-advancement or a self-indulgent lifestyle.

Blessings. Have a great day.

Day Eighty-One

Mark 12:28–44

Hello Lucas,

A religious leader asked Jesus which was the greatest commandment. Jesus said, "Love the Lord your God with all your heart and with all your soul and with all your mind and with all your strength," and "Love your neighbor as yourself." If you love God and others, you will not want to harm them in any way. Therefore, if you walk in love, you will not be breaking the other commandments (stealing, lying, killing, etc.).

When God commands you to love Him whole heartedly, you must ask the question, "Can anyone love on command?" You will find that love is only possible by building relationships. Your love for others grows as you spend time with them and build relationships. Likewise with God. He wants you to enter into a personal relationship with Him so that your love can have a chance to develop. This is not accomplished through religious ceremonies, duties, or activities but through developing an intimate relationship.

Lucas, take God out of the "religious box" and treat Him like your closest friend, then watch your love grow for God and others.

Blessings. Have a great day.

Day Eighty-Two

Mark 13:1–20

Hello Lucas,

Jesus will return and rule as King out of Jerusalem for one thousand years. He tells His disciples what world events take place right before His return. In verse 14, He describes a major political and religious event that happens very close to His return. This event is so notable that Jesus, Daniel, Paul, Matthew, Mark, and John all mention it in relation to Christ's return.

BACKDROP FOR THE EVENT

1. A ten-nation coalition forms to rule the world, possibly the UN or some other political union.
2. A world leader arises called the Antichrist.
3. A cashless society is instituted that requires people to receive the "mark of beast," possibly a computer chip.
4. A seven-year peace treaty is made between Israel and the world leader.
5. Israel rebuilds its temple.

THE ACTUAL EVENT

1. Three and a half years before Christ returns, the Antichrist sets an idol of himself in the temple at Jerusalem and demands that everyone worship it.
2. The Antichrist world leader destroys Jerusalem, kills many Jews, and crushes Christians.

Lucas, Jesus has told you these things so that you will know ahead and have peace and so that you will not be deceived by fake Christs, fake religions, and the end-time "political beast."

Blessings. Have a great day.

Day Eighty-Three

Mark 13:21–37

Hello Lucas,

Christians can get confused about Jesus's return. In one place, Paul corrected some believers who were saying that Jesus had already returned. Others think that Jesus will secretly come and catch them away before returning.

Jesus clarifies all of that in verse 21 by saying that His return will not be a secret thing seen by only a few. In verse 22, He warns that imposters will come claiming to be Him and that fake prophets will come and do miracles that deceive many.

In verse 24, He describes the final sign—a great cosmic disturbance, a massive meteor shower, and the darkening of the sun and moon. Then Jesus will return in the clouds in all His power and glory. At that time, Christians will be brought to life and be caught up to meet Him as He returns in the clouds. Remember when Jesus ascended to heaven? The angel told the disciples, "This same Jesus, who has been taken from you into heaven, will come back in the same way you have seen him go into heaven" (Acts 1:11).

Jesus is coming again from heaven in the clouds. It will be a big event that everyone will see, and He will call you to His side. That is the joy awaiting you!

Blessings. Have a great day.

Day Eighty-Four

Mark 14:1–31

Hello Lucas,

In a few days, Jesus will suffer and die. So He is taking every opportunity to prepare His followers ahead of time. When a woman anoints Him with costly perfume, He explains that it is in preparation for His coming burial. Then when they are celebrating the Passover dinner, He tells them that one of them (Judas) will hand Him over to be killed. He explains that His blood will be shed to wash away the sins of the world. He predicts that He will be dragged off and that all of His disciples will run away and that Peter will deny knowing Him.

Jesus foretells all these events so that you will know that these things were planned by God. Satan wanted to kill Jesus out of jealously and hatred, but God used that to fulfill His own salvation plan.

God has special plans for your life, and sometimes Satan tries to disturb them. But God always takes what the enemy means for evil and turns it for good.

Blessings. Have a great day.

Day Eighty-Five

Mark 14:32–72

Hello Lucas,

It was nighttime when Jesus led His disciples to a secluded garden. His soul was deeply distressed because He knew how much He would suffer. He prayed, asking God if there was any backup plan available. Deep inside, He knew that suffering was the only way to pay for your sin. After wrestling in prayer, He made this amazing statement to God: "Yet not what I will, but what you will." Within minutes, He was arrested, led to a mock trial, and then abused

Jesus gave up His will in order to submit to God's plan and will. He took the punishment for your sin so that you could have peace with God. That is called "redemptive suffering."

Sometimes it is God's plan that you suffer things from people because you love Jesus. Like Jesus, you should consider these sufferings worth it, knowing that God will use your "redemptive suffering" so that others can find peace with God. Like Jesus, just pray and surrender your will.

Blessings. Have a great day.

Day Eighty-Six

Mark 15:1–20

Hello Lucas,

While standing trial before the religious leaders, Jesus gave witness that He was the Son of God. Early in the morning, He was brought before Pilate, the Roman political leader, where He confessed that He was the King from heaven. They beat Him and led Him away to be crucified. While facing death, He did not falter but spoke the truth. In doing so, He fulfilled God's plan and made a way for many people to enter heaven.

In 2002, at Namphainong, Arunachal Pradesh, India, one of our new believers was told by radical Hindus, "Either deny Jesus and return to Hinduism, or we will chop you to pieces with daos" (a utility machete). He said, "I cannot deny Jesus whom I have seen." He died a terrible death.

Sinners will never be free unless they hear the truth. Jesus came to bear witness to the truth. Like Him, you must be ready to give your testimony of the truth that Jesus is both King and Lord. He is the only Son of the living God.

Blessings. Have a great day.

Day Eighty-Seven

Mark 15:21–47

Hello Lucas,

The crucifixion, suffering, and death of Jesus was a public show that everyone watched. Most of the religious and political leaders, the military, the general public, and even His followers gave witness to His death.

Why did God subject His Son to a public demonstration of humiliation at the hands of sinners as He laid down His life in death? Paul explains, "But God demonstrates his own love for us in this: While we were still sinners, Christ died for us" (Romans 5:8). God loved us so much that He was prepared to suffer in order to be near us.

This is what that same love of God will look like as you allow it to grow within your life:

You will be kinder and more patient.

You will not be envious of others or boastful.

You will not be proud, rude, or self-seeking.

You will not be easily angered.

You will not keep a record of the wrong things that others have done to you.

You will not delight in evil but rejoice with the truth.

You will always protect, always trust, always hope, and always persevere.

You will never fail.

Blessings. Have a great day.

Day Eighty-Eight

Mark 16:1–8

Hello Lucas,

On Friday, Jesus was placed in the tomb. Some of the ladies who followed Him saw this and wanted to bring burial spices. Because of the religious holiday, they had to wait until Sunday morning, but by then it was too late; Jesus had risen. An angel met them, saying, "He has risen! . . . Go, tell his disciples and Peter." They were shocked to see all this, but they went ahead and told the other disciples.

From the beginning of time, God had promised that His Son would rise from the dead.

Notice that the angel added, "Tell Peter." Why was that important? Because as Jesus was suffering, Peter denied knowing Jesus. Even though Peter failed God at a critical time, God knew ahead. Jesus wanted to meet Peter right away so that He could restore their relationship.

You have entered a kingdom based on redemption and restoration. God has called you so that He can pay for every one of your fallen situations and restore all that is broken within you. You have a loving and kind Savior. If you fail Him, He is doing everything in His power to bring you back to the right place. Always be quick to return.

Blessings. Have a great day.

Day Eighty-Nine

Mark 16:9–20

Hello Lucas,

Jesus rose from the grave and first appeared to some of the ladies who were His followers. One of them, Mary Magdalene, was previously delivered from demon possession and had a really messed up life. He showed Himself alive first to the common person, not the high in society. In doing so, He showed that there is no difference between man or woman, upper class or lower class. n Him all are valued and equal.

Others told the disciples that Jesus was alive, but they did not believe it. So in verse 14, Jesus appeared to them and challenged their lack of faith. He commanded them, "Go into all the world and preach the gospel to all creation."

The current global population is 7.9 billion people, and about 34 percent of them have become Christian. But still 1.6 billion have never heard about Jesus. Each day, 30 million people go to the grave without hearing the Gospel.

You must do everything in your power to fulfill this final command of Jesus so that the people of your generation can know the love that God has for them.

Blessings. Have a great day.

CHAPTER FOUR

Luke

Day Ninety

Luke 1:1–38

Hello Lucas,

Luke was led by God to interview eyewitnesses and write an orderly account of Jesus's life for a new believer named Theophilus. He begins the account by telling the story of a prophet that God promised to send right before sending His Son, Jesus. Luke gives the account of John the Baptist's birth, showing that John was that promised forerunner-prophet, as the angel clearly states in verse 17. "See, I will send the prophet Elijah to you before that great and dreadful day of the LORD comes. He will turn the hearts of the parents to their children, and the hearts of the children to their parents; or else I will come and strike the land with total destruction" (Malachi 4:5–6).

In verses 26–27, the same angel, Gabriel, appears to a virgin girl named Mary and announces that she will give birth to the Son of God. After asking a couple of questions, she says, "May your word to me be fulfilled."

Luke researched these things and recorded them so that we could know for certain what happened.

From this, you can see that God has encircled the whole world with His wonderful plan. When He interrupts your life by introducing His plan for it, just respond the same way Mary did: "May your word to me be fulfilled." Then watch the amazing things that God does with you.

Blessings. Have a great day!

Day Ninety-One

Luke 1:39–80

Hello Lucas,

In the births of Jesus and John the Baptist we see a plan that only God could arrange. Mary conceived Jesus without a sexual relationship, and Elizabeth, who was a barren old woman, gave birth to John the Baptist. Jesus came from the kingly tribe of Judah, so He could legally become King of the Jews. And John was from the priestly tribe of Levi, so he could endorse Jesus's new priestly order.

Mary and Elizabeth were related, so they met together and rejoiced. Notice the powerful presence of the Holy Spirit as accounted for in these verses:

15. John was filled with the Holy Spirit in his mother's womb.
35. The Holy Spirit would bring the power of God for Mary to conceive.
41. Elizabeth, filled with the Holy Spirit, blessed Mary.
46. Mary, full of the Holy Spirit, prophesied and rejoiced.
67. John's father, Zechariah, filled with the Holy Spirit, prophesied.

The Holy Spirit is the person of God who brings power to accomplish His plans upon the earth. Lucas, allow the presence of His Spirit to move in your life as well.

Blessings. Have a great day.

Day Ninety-Two

Luke 2:1–40

Hello Lucas,

In researching the birth of Jesus, Luke linked it to the first Roman census under Quirinius, showing that it was an actual historical event. That census required Mary and Joseph to travel and be counted in Joseph's ancestral village, Bethlehem. In doing so, that event caused Jesus to be born in Bethlehem, which fulfilled the prophetic promise that "Out of you [Bethlehem] will come for me one who will be ruler over Israel, whose origins are from of old, from ancient times" (Micah 5:2).

In verses 8–13, a group of angels appeared to the local shepherds, announcing the birth of Jesus. After going to see Jesus, the shepherds went everywhere testifying that the things the angels said would happen did happen. When Joseph and Mary took Jesus to the temple for His circumcision and dedication, a godly man there prophesied that Jesus was the Savior promised hundreds of years earlier. "I will keep you and will make you to be a covenant for the people and a light for the Gentiles" (Isaiah 42:6). Also, an eighty-four-year-old woman, a prophetess, told the people that Jesus was the Redeemer sent from God.

God has given you an accurate historical, prophetic, and personal testimony so that you may know for certain that Jesus is His promised Son.

Blessings. Have a great day.

Day Ninety-Three

Luke 2:41–52

Hello Lucas,

At age twelve, Jesus went to Jerusalem with His parents for the Passover feast. Returning home, they saw that Jesus was missing. Several days later, they found Him in the temple, discussing scriptures with the religious teachers. All were amazed at His understanding and answers. When His parents scolded Him, He replied, "Didn't you know I had to be in my Father's house?"

Jesus knew that His Father was God and that He had a heavenly purpose. He also understood that it was not yet time for His public ministry to begin. It was still time for Him to submit to His parents. So it says that "he went . . . with them and was obedient to them."

This is the only story of Jesus's childhood that was recorded. What was so important about it that God had it recorded? It was Jesus's lifestyle of obedient submission to God's plan that purchased your salvation.

You can see through Jesus's example that God's power in your life is most effective when you obediently submit to His plans. I regularly ask God to give me a willing and obedient heart.

Blessings. Have a great day.

Day Ninety-Four

Luke 3:1–20

Hello Lucas,

John the Baptist was living in the desert, awaiting God's direction to begin his public ministry. Luke names the political and religious leaders that were in office once John began. In addition, he explains how John's ministry was also foretold by Isaiah the prophet.

Here's the message John gave:

1. A time of God's wrath is coming.
2. Repent and turn away from your sins.
3. Prove your repentance by showing a changed lifestyle.
4. Be baptized in water.
5. Sinners will be cast into the fire.
6. I baptize with water, but Christ will baptize you with the Holy Spirit.
7. Christ will refine His followers and burn up the sinner.

John gave a message of repentance but did not personally have the power to make a complete change within people's hearts. He explained that Christ would come and fill people with the Holy Spirit, then the work and fire of the Holy Spirit would change people from the inside out.

Lucas, always cooperate with the Holy Spirit as He works to clean your heart and mind.

Blessings. Have a great day.

Day Ninety-Five

Luke 3:21–38

Hello Lucas,

As John the Baptist preached about repentance and the coming Messiah, those who believed were baptized. In verse 21, Jesus also came to be baptized. Since Jesus had not sinned, why was it important that He get baptized? And why did He say in Matthew 3:15, "It is proper for us to do this to fulfill all righteousness"? There are several probable reasons:

1. His heavenly Father told Him to.
2. He carried our sins for us in the body as a man on the cross and symbolically died to them in baptism.
3. Sharing our humanity, He left the example for us to repent and be baptized.
4. Ceremonial cleansing was required under the law to enter priesthood.
5. This made it possible for John to introduce Jesus publicly as the Messiah.
6. God affirmed audibly and publicly that Jesus was His Son.

After baptism, Jesus began His public ministry.

Luke also gives Jesus's genealogy through His adopted father's side (Joseph), showing that He qualified as king by royal birth.

Blessings. Have a great day.

Day Ninety-Six

Luke 4:1–13

Hello Lucas,

God created man and gave him authority over all the earth, but Satan stole it by tempting the first man, Adam. In order to legally restore mankind, Jesus had to be tempted as a man in every way by Satan but without sinning. In verse 6, Satan said he would give Jesus all the authority of the world's kingdoms if He worshipped him. It was a legitimate offer to redeem the world without suffering. Satan is a liar and would not have honored anything, but the test was real. Jesus endured forty days of temptations without sinning and won a major battle in restoring man's authority and position with God, which Adam had originally lost.

Jesus left the desert and began His public ministry. As He did, the people were amazed that He taught with authority and had authority to cast out devils and heal the sick.

All authority in heaven and earth was purchased by Jesus, and He has given that authority back to you, Lucas. Move forward in that authority to undo the mess that Satan has made in the world around you.

Blessings. Have a great day.

Day Ninety-Seven

Luke 4:14–44

Hello Lucas,

Jesus went from village to village ministering in the power of the Holy Spirit. Everywhere He went, He healed the sick, cast out evil spirits, and taught with great authority. Each Sabbath, Saturday, He would enter the local synagogue (Jewish church) and teach. One week, He did this in His own hometown, but the people there would not receive His ministry, because He was their neighbor. So He told them that the prophets Elijah and Elisha were not honored by their neighbors either.

In all the other villages, multitudes were receiving healing and deliverance, but in Nazareth (Jesus's village), the people received nothing from Him.

From this you can learn two lessons:

1. If God is doing something great around you, don't miss out because the presentation or person offends you.
2. Even though you may look like an average person to some, God can still use you to minister powerfully to others.

Blessings. Have a great day.

Day Ninety-Eight

Luke 5:1–11

Hello Lucas,

Many people come to the Lord during a crisis. They live life distanced from God until things fall apart. Once they let Him in, He picks up the pieces, puts them back together, and gives them an amazing destiny. God had good plans all along, He just had to get their attention.

That's what happened when Jesus called Peter, Andrew, James, and John to be disciples. Their fishing business wasn't producing, so they let Jesus use a boat so that He could teach the crowds from it. Afterward, Jesus took them out in the sea and filled their nets so full that both boats almost sank.

In verse 10, He told Peter, "From now on you will fish for people."

Notice their response: They "left everything and followed him." The fish that Peter was trying so desperately to catch meant nothing once He encountered the reality of Jesus.

Likewise, now that you have personally experienced God, all other things will fade in comparison. Your destiny in Him will be all that matters.

Blessings. Have a great day.

Day Ninety-Nine

Luke 5:12–39

Hello Lucas,

A man with leprosy (skin disease) humbly came to Jesus, saying, "If you are willing, you can make me clean." Jesus immediately healed him. From this we see that God is always willing to do good for people, they only need to ask.

Then some men carried a paralyzed friend to Jesus for healing. He not only healed him but loudly proclaimed, "Your sins are forgiven." From this we see that God wants to do more than we expect. Ephesians 3:20 says, "To him who is able to do immeasurably more than all we ask or imagine."

Then Jesus called a tax collector to be His disciple. Notice the tax collector's response. "Levi got up, left everything and followed him."

God has also called you to be His disciple. Like Levi, you chose to leave everything that stood in the way, so that you can spread the kindness and generosity of God into the lives of others.

Blessings. Have a great day.

Day One Hundred

Luke 6:1–11

Hello Lucas,

Jesus dealt with the religious leaders concerning their day of worship—the "Sabbath." When God created the heavens and the earth, He rested on the seventh day, blessed it, and called it holy. He wanted it to be a blessing whereby men could rest from their labor each week, just as He rested after creation. Instead, the religious leaders created many laws around it that overburdened the people. Jesus corrected them, showing that it was lawful to do good works on the Sabbath. He explained further, saying that He was "Lord of the Sabbath." In saying this, He showed that He was with God in the beginning, and as Creator, He was Lord of all things.

The Sabbath symbolized the coming of the Messiah (Jesus), who would provide a permanent spiritual rest for God's people. Jesus's life and death purchased your spiritual rest. You do not have to perform religious works to enter God's kingdom. You only have to obey God and then rest in the finished work of Jesus. Hallelujah!

Blessings. Have a great day.

Day One Hundred One

Luke 6:12–49

Hello Lucas,

Christianity is not a religious idea thought up by one person. Goc has always foretold His plans and documented their completion by the testimony of eyewitnesses. That's why He called twelve men (the apostles) to be witnesses to the ife and ministry of Jesus.

After that, Jesus healed many people and taught the crowds how things work in the kingdom of God.

1. God gives blessings to you when you suffer these difficult situations: poverty, hunger, grief, rejection, being hated, and being insulted.
2. As His son, you should respond in love to unlovely people.
3. You are to judge others for the sake of evaluation and restoration, not to condemn them.
4. You are to forgive others generously.

He explained that when someone is truly in His kingdom, good things will come from their heart. And if someone truly loves Him, they will do what He says.

By faith you have entered God's kingdom. Continue to love and obey Him so that people will see. Every true spiritual child will look like their heavenly Father; every disciplined student will be like his teacher; and every good tree produces good fruit. Let that be your story.

Blessings. Have a great day.

Day One Hundred Two

Luke 7:1–17

Hello Lucas,

Is it possible that your faith can save or change the destiny of someone else's life for the good? One day a centurion (military commander of six thousand) humbly requested that Jesus heal his valued servant who was almost dead. Jesus marveled at the man's faith-filled words and said, "I tell you, I have not found such great faith even in Israel." As a result, the servant was completely healed. The servant was healed because of the commander's faith. Then Jesus went on to cure many who had diseases, sicknesses, and evil spirits. He gave sight to the blind and brought a dead boy back to life. Verse 13 tells us what motivated Him—He was moved with compassion.

Imagine this with me: You know someone who will die shortly. Your heart goes out to them, and you cry in prayer, "God I believe that you can heal them." Then God does. If you had not expressed faith and compassion, that person would be dead. You changed their destiny for the good!

Lucas, if you move forward with compassion and great faith, you will see people around you delivered both physically, spiritually, and emotionally.

Blessings. Have a great day.

Day One Hundred Three

Luke 7:18–50

Hello Lucas,

John the Baptist prepared the way for Jesus by preaching to the people, by baptizing Him, and by publicly confessing that Jesus was the Messiah. But in verse 18, John sent some of his disciples to ask Jesus, "Are you the one who was to come, or should we expect someone else?" Now that John was in prison and facing death, doubts were entering his heart. Jesus sent this message back to John: "Blessed is anyone who does not stumble on account of me."

Later, a woman who had been forgiven of a very sinful lifestyle brought a gift to show her appreciation to Jesus. People judged and opposed her, but Jesus defended her, affirming that her sins were forgiven.

Standing up for Jesus is easy when life is going smoothly, but when persecution or opposition comes, people often become offended and fall away. Be determined ahead of time to stand strong when things get tough and confusing. Always remember the encouraging words of Jesus, "The one who stands firm to the end will be saved" (Matthew 24:13).

Blessings. Have a great day.

Day One Hundred Four

Luke 8:1–39

Hello Lucas,

The world is always rejecting God, and for two thousand years it has been trying to stamp out Christianity. While King Herod tried to silence the message by killing John the Baptist, some of his own royal attendants accepted Christ. In verse 3, Luke documents one of them named Joanna, who also later witnessed the resurrection of Jesus.

Jesus taught about the kingdom of God, comparing it to a farmer planting seed, saying that if you hold on to the seed of God's Word with a good heart, you will produce a good harvest. Whoever grows in God's kingdom and produces fruit will be entrusted with more. He said that you are His family if you hear and practice His words.

This is the way that God has been advancing His kingdom throughout the whole world. Even though the world has tried to stop God's kingdom, Christianity has grown to be the largest religion in the world. You are a part of that great kingdom.

Blessings. Have a great day.

Day One Hundred Five

Luke 8:40–56

Hello Lucas,

Jesus continued His mission of healing, deliverance, and teaching. He healed a woman with a twelve-year bleeding issue and raised a young girl from the dead.

Around 2004, my team and I experienced these same two miracles We were holding the first ever Healing Festival in Nafra, India, among the Miji people. Their system of worship included daily animal sacrifice. Their high priest's wife had been bleeding every day for twelve years. When she was prayed for in Jesus's name, she was healed. When I asked the high priest if he knew about Jesus, God's Son, he said, "I don't know much about Jesus Christ, but when my wife was prayed for in Jesus's name and healed, I realized that there was something much bigger than I knew."

At that same meeting, a woman brought her young daughter. Pressing through the crowd, she said, "Three of my four daughters have died, from the eldest to the youngest, and tonight my last one has died. When we checked, the girl had no breath or pulse. As we prayed for her in Jesus's name, she immediately came to life. When the people saw these things, many accepted Jesus, even the high priest's wife.

Lucas, Jesus promised you that "Whoever believes in me . . . will do even greater things than these" (John 14:12). Let your life bring glory to God this same way that Jesus did!

Blessings. Have a great day.

Day One Hundred Six

Luke 9:1–17

Hello Lucas,

Jesus called His twelve disciples together and sent them out to minister like He was doing. Before they left, He surprised them by saying, "Take nothing for the journey—no staff, no bag, no bread, no money, no extra shirt." Jesus wanted them to learn that God would miraculously provide for their every need. They returned rejoicing at the success of the ministry and provision.

This is a very important lesson. If God has called you to do some ministry or outreach, He will provide all that is needed. You do not have to wait for every detail and dollar before obeying.

In verse 13, Jesus told the disciples to feed five thousand people with five loaves of bread and two fish. To help their faith, He had the people sit down in groups of fifty. As they gave food to the fifty, there was still enough for the next fifty and so on until all were fed.

Lucas, if you do not have faith to provide for one hundred people, begin by helping the first two. By the time you come to the next two, God will have miraculously provided more.

Like the disciples, Jesus sends you out to do His ministry among the people, and He will provide for you.

Blessings. Have a great day.

Day One Hundred Seven

Luke 9:18–62

Hello Lucas,

Everywhere Jesus went, He continued to teach how to live in the kingdom of God:

1. You die daily to your self-centered life and follow Jesus and His agenda.
2. If you are ashamed of Him and His teachings, He will be ashamed of you when He returns.
3. To do His miracles, your belief in His ability must surpass your doubts.
4. Serving others without seeking recognition is more honorable than being the "top man."
5. There is a cost for following Jesus.
6. You carry the message of the kingdom to others.
7. You cannot look back to the old life.

Every nation has its culture and customs; some are good, and some are bad. You can no longer justify living the wrong lifestyle by saying, "Our culture accepts it." Through faith in Jesus, you have entered the kingdom of God. As a heavenly citizen, you now live by its culture and customs.

Lucas, intentionally and joyfully live the kingdom culture.

Blessings. Have a great day.

Day One Hundred Eight

Luke 10:1–17

Hello Lucas,

Jesus said, "The harvest is plentiful, but the workers are few." Then He sent seventy-two of His followers to the villages to minister to the people. Here we see that Jesus wants to reach the whole field (world) and has appointed us to do it. He showed an effective way to reach people:

1. Meet others and find a person with a peaceful disposition.
2. Build a relationship with that family and fellowship with them.
3. Minister to their physical and spiritual needs.
4. Tell them about God and His kingdom and the Gospel.
5. If they will not receive you, don't take it personally; it is actually Jesus whom they are rejecting.

According to Jesus, there are not enough servants willing or ready to work in the field.

Since you love Him, you want to help Him reach and harvest the lost. You can begin by reaching out to one person, using these simple steps that He left.

Blessings. Have a great day.

Day One Hundred Nine

Luke 10:18–42

Hello Lucas,

Jesus's disciples were understanding what He taught and were effectively ministering to others. When Jesus saw this, verse 21 says He was "full of joy," and excitedly thanked God for showing spiritual truth to His children. The world thinks that God is angry, impersonal, distant, and only judgmental. But here we see otherwise. We can fill His heart with joy. Like a proud parent, He says, "That's my boy!" "That's my girl!"

Jesus went on to teach a religious leader that helping others in their time of need is true love. After that, He went to the house of Martha and Mary, a couple of His close followers. Martha was preparing food and was upset because Mary was sitting, listening to Jesus teach instead of helping her. As Martha complained, Jesus said, "Indeed only one thing is needed. Mary has chosen what is better." From this we learn that there will never be an end of things to do. The best thing that we can do is to set aside unnecessary things and spend time with the Lord.

For as long as my wife and I have been married, we get up each morning and spend about an hour with each other, reading God's Word and praying. Doing that really sets our day on a good trajectory. On days that we miss, we can feel the world creeping in on us.

Lucas, think about ways that you can spend more time with Jesus each week.

Blessings. Have a great day.

Day One Hundred Ten

Luke 11:1–11

Hello Lucas,

Prayer is one of the most powerful tools and weapons that you have.

Jesus taught the following:

1. The pattern for prayer
2. To be persistent
3. To ask, expecting to get an answer
4. To seek, looking to find the answer
5. To knock until you receive the answer
6. To know that you will receive the answer
7. To ask for the Holy Spirit

This is how it works:

When you pray, your prayers ascend to heaven and are collected into bowls. Incense and fire from God's altar is mixed with them as an aroma before God. At the perfect time, an angel casts your answer to earth and it arrives. That is described in Revelation 8:3–5.

Even though Jesus was the Son of God, in order to minister effectively in the flesh, He prayed daily. If He needed to pray, how much more do you need to? As you pray, the Holy Spirit will stir your heart with the emotions and compassion of God. He will bring words to your mind so that you can pray the perfect will of God for individual situations and people. God will answer in the perfect time. Don't give up!

Blessings. Have a great day.

Day One Hundred Eleven

Luke 11:12–54

Hello Lucas,

Jesus taught about spiritual warfare:

1. In order to drive the evil out of a man, someone stronger must come into his life. To keep that person clean, someone stronger must remain within him. This is why we accept Jesus into our lives and allow the Holy Spirit to fill us daily.
2. Our eye is a powerful gateway into our spirit. If we look at evil things, our spirit will be overcome with darkness. Set your eyes and desires on godly things so that your spirit shines brightly.
3. Outward religious rules and appearances do not bring spiritual power. It's like being clothed in full military dress without having a single weapon. Acting on and doing the words of God is the weapon that defeats the enemy and brings true inner, spiritual change.

You are a soldier in God's army, fighting to free people from the forces of darkness and bondage. Make sure that you understand and use His spiritual weapons properly so that you can effectively help others.

Blessings. Have a great day.

Day One Hundred Twelve

Luke 12:1–34

Hello Lucas,

Every parent knows how foolish it is to let a child go his own way unhindered. We place healthy boundaries and hold our children accountable because we love them. Likewise, as God's children, each one of us will stand before Him and give an account of our life. Jesus explains some of our boundaries and shows us that we need to develop a healthy fear of the Lord.

In verses 14–34 Jesus teaches you to

1. guard against greed,
2. be rich in godly things,
3. refuse to stress over material things,
4. seek His kingdom first, and He will provide for all your needs,
5. store up treasures in heaven, and
6. choose heavenly possessions over earthly possessions, because your heart ends up attached to your possessions.

Proverbs 1:7 says, "The fear of the LORD is the beginning of knowledge." As God's child, you have enjoyed His grace and forgiveness. Now that you are maturing, you should also respect and fear Him.

Blessings. Have a great day.

Day One Hundred Thirteen

Luke 12:35–59

Hello Lucas,

Jesus came into this world as Suffering Servant and promised to return later as ruling King. Whenever someone leaves for a prolonged time, we tend to lose interest and become distracted, and the relationship cools. Jesus, knowing human nature, warned His followers about this and left instructions:

1. Live in anticipation of His return every day.
2. Serve faithfully in His absence.
3. Keep your spiritual lamp burning.
4. Be ready because He will come unexpectedly.
5. If you do not prepare for His coming and begin living like the world, you will be placed among the unbelievers.
6. You have been given much, and He expects you to bring others to Him.

In verse 49, He calls every believer into a deeper commitment of "fiery love" and explains that some family members will reject you because of Him.

Since you know these things, eagerly await His return, faithfully serve, and don't let your love for Him grow cold.

Blessings. Have a great day.

Day One Hundred Fourteen

Luke 13:1–17

Hello Lucas,

Sometimes people suffer tragedy and others say, "They are getting what they deserve because they are wicked." That's what happened here. Someone told Jesus about several people who were executed. So He took the opportunity to teach them that all have sinned, not just those suffering or being caught. He said everyone must repent or perish eternally.

He told a story about the owner of a tree that didn't bear fruit for three years. The owner gave the order to cut it down, and the gardener requested one final year to nurture and hopefully make it produce.

Jesus taught a lot about repentance (turning from our sin). In this story, we see Him giving people a period of time to repent and produce a good, fruitful life. All of us would do well to respond before our designated time runs out.

In verse 10, a crippled woman afflicted by a demon was at worship service, and Jesus healed her. The religious leader corrected Jesus for disturbing the meeting. Jesus corrected him for caring more about himself than helping the afflicted.

Lucas, do not approach your spiritual life in a haphazard, ineffective, and unproductive way. God is doing all that He can to help you produce good spiritual fruit; be sure to cooperate with that process.

Blessings. Have a great day.

Day One Hundred Fifteen

Luke 13:18–35

Hello Lucas,

Jesus continued teaching about the kingdom of God:

1. It came to us through Jesus, who was the originating "smallest seed." He predicted that it would become the largest plant, where people could find rest. So many people have accepted Jesus that Christianity is now the largest world religion.
2. Its entry door is narrow (through Jesus and obeying Him).
3. Many will not make it in because they do evil.
4. You must make every effort to enter.
5. Your opportunity to enter is limited. You must choose now while still alive.
6. Evildoers will enter hell and will be cast away from the kingdom into eternal torment.

In verse 34, Jesus cried deeply over the people and city of Jerusalem for rejecting Him and God's kingdom. Second Peter 3:9 gives us a similar glimpse into the heart of God: "He is patient with you, not wanting anyone to perish, but everyone to come to repentance." Often people only focus on the judgments that God has to execute. We need to realize that His compassion is so great that He weeps over every soul who chooses to reject Him.

Lucas, the kingdom of God is a place of hope; continue to help others find the door.

Blessings. Have a great day.

Day One Hundred Sixteen

Luke 14:1–24

Hello Lucas,

Jesus was invited to a banquet and used the opportunity to teach about true love, compassion, humility, and benevolent kindness. He said if we do these things God will honor and reward us at the resurrection.

He also told a story about the "large banquet" that God will give. In the story, God invites everyone to His kingdom and banquet. Many people are busy with life and make all kinds of excuses for not going. He is upset that they refuse their opportunity. So He sends messengers everywhere inviting even the sick and handicapped (the spiritually unqualified). Finally, He sends more workers out to the most remote areas, saying, "Compel them to come in, so that my house will be full."

God's love for mankind is so great that He wants as many people as possible to enter His house eternally. I have heard some people say, "Religion is a private thing, and I don't want to talk about it." Jesus knew that many people would have that attitude and end up in hell. Jesus told this story so that you would understand the urgency of "compelling" others to Him. You must make every effort and use every means possible to draw others into eternal life.

Blessings. Have a great day.

Day One Hundred Seventeen

Luke 14:25–35

Hello Lucas,

This earthly life is short, but we often live as though it is all that exists. When someone near us dies, the reality of eternity faces us. Coming from heaven, Jesus always lived and taught from an eternal perspective. In verse 25, He made that very point by saying that anyone who wants to be His (eternal) disciple must hate his (earthly) life, die to his own (earthly) desires, and be willing to give up everything and follow Him.

In the original language of the New Testament, the word Jesus used that is translated into English as "hate" has a more specific meaning: to "love less." There is a cost to entering the kingdom of God and following Jesus. The cost is obedience. It is loving our temporary life less so that we can have eternal life. The things that seem so important to you now will often mean little to you a few years later. If you give your full attention and energy mainly to earthly things, you will find out later that your life was spent on things your hands cannot hold on to.

Lucas, continue giving it all to Jesus and follow Him. He is the way to eternal life.

Blessings. Have a great day.

Day One Hundred Eighteen

Luke 15:1–10

Hello Lucas,

Jesus showed His great concern for sinful and unlovely people by associating with them. When the religious leaders insulted Him for it, He told two stories showing that the lost need to be found. If you have ever lost your phone or wallet, you remember the frantic search retracing your steps until it was found. When you find it, there is a great sense of relief, and you rejoice.

Jesus said that's the way it is in heaven. Notice in both stories, when a lost sinner repents, everyone in heaven gets excited and rejoices. Imagine that angels are happy, saying, "Look, he finally made it. He's going to be with us forever. Satan lost another one. Woohoo!" Yes, God is that happy over one person repenting.

As a Christian, you should not approve of sin. However, you still associate with sinners so that you can help them find God. At the same time, be careful not to let them draw you back into sin. If you are hanging with people that influence you into sin, it is best to leave them until you are stronger in the Lord.

Blessings. Have a great day.

Day One Hundred Nineteen

Luke 15:11–32

Hello Lucas,

Jesus continues to explain God's concern for the lost. He tells a story of a wayward son who ran off and partied away his inheritance. Poor and destitute, the son headed home.

Look at the son's response:

1. I have sinned against heaven and you. (He took responsibility for his actions.)
2. I am not worthy to be your son. (He was sincere and humbled himself.)

Look at the father's response:

1. He was eagerly watching from afar.
2. He was filled with compassion.
3. He gave a hug (full acceptance), a kiss (full affection), the best clothes (clean covering instead of filthy), a family ring (royal identity and authority), shoes (ability to walk right), and a feast (satisfied and celebrating).

When the older brother questioned the father's generosity, he explained, "This brother of yours was dead and is alive again; he was lost and is found."

Although people are lost and spiritually dead, the loving heavenly Father waits to greet them in the same generous way. Maybe some of those same lost people consider themselves your enemies. If they do turn to God and repent, don't question His generosity, just celebrate along with God, since another lost one has been found.

Blessings. Have a great day.

Day One Hundred Twenty

Luke 16:1–15

Hello Lucas,

Jesus taught His disciples how to use money properly. He told the story of a worldly man who used money to make friends. He went on to explain that the world uses finances to advance themselves on earth and that Christians should use finances to advance themselves in eternity.

This is what He said:

1. Use earthly money to get others into heaven eternally (verse 9).
2. If you are faithful with little, you will be trusted with much (verse 10).
3. Use earthly wealth correctly, and you will be trusted with true spiritual wealth (verse 11).
4. All that you have is on loan from God; use it for Him (verse 12).
5. You can't serve God and focus mainly on worldly wealth (verse 13).

Jesus said something shocking regarding this issue: "The people of this world are more shrewd in dealing with their own kind than are the people of light."

As a Christian, you want to be wiser than the world. You need to take the responsibility of finances seriously. The way you handle money will reflect how well you will manage your spiritual life and resources. If you are not trustworthy with money, you will not be trustworthy with spiritual things either.

Lucas, use money to serve God; don't serve money and use God.

Blessings. Have a great day.

Day One Hundred Twenty-One

Luke 16:16–31

Hello Lucas,

While teaching on money, Jesus talked about a rich man who ignored God and did not help the needy. That man ended up in hell. Today, people avoid the topic of hell, but Jesus taught more about it than heaven. Why? Because He wants everyone to avoid it. Jesus taught about hell at least seventy times.

In this story, what did He say about hell?

1. It is a hot place full of suffering.
2. All have sinned and are headed there.
3. The only way to avoid it is to believe in Jesus and repent.
4. Each person is given a space of time to repent.
5. God has given us sufficient warning.
6. Once you are in hell, it's too late.
7. There is no passage between hell to heaven.

When my nephew was a toddler learning to walk, he ran straight to the stove. Everyone in the room yelled for him to stop, but he didn't. He placed his hands on the hot stove and pulled back ten blistered fingers. After the shock left his face, he cried profusely. Everyone in the room felt terrible.

Likewise, your loving heavenly Father has warned you ahead, so you can avoid hell's fire.

Blessings. Have a great day.

Day One Hundred Twenty-Two

Luke 17:1–19

Hello Lucas,

Here is an interesting but fearful thought: We can draw someone away from sin or drag them deeper into it. That's why Jesus said it would be better for a person to drown than to cause a child to sin. God will judge us if we lead others into sin.

He goes on to explain the importance of forgiving the person who is truly sorry but keeps failing. Some people are sincere but have not overcome their issues yet. This does not mean that we enable their bad behavior. We may have to close some doors and put up boundaries so they have less of a chance to offend, but our love for them remains, and we forgive them from our hearts.

In verses 11–14, Jesus heals ten men of skin disease. Only one returns to give thanks. People are often looking to God for an answer but quickly forget Him afterward. How often do they remember or thank Him once things are going well?

Lucas, influence others for the good, always be ready to forgive, and always give thanks to God for His kindness.

Blessings. Have a great day.

Day One Hundred Twenty-Three

Luke 17:20–37

Hello Lucas,

The religious leaders knew that the Messiah would come and set up God's kingdom on earth, so they asked Jesus when that would happen. He said that you won't find it by looking here or there and finding it in a physical location. Instead, He told them that God would first establish it within the hearts of men. Then He explained what things would be like on earth just before He returns to set up the kingdom on earth:

1. People will be like they were when Noah was building the ark. They ignored Noah's warning and continued life as usual, then the flood came unexpectedly and destroyed them.
2. It will be sudden, like the meteor shower that destroyed Sodom and took the people by surprise.

Right now, God is building His kingdom within us. Soon, Jesus will return and establish it on earth.

Lucas, allow God to continue building His kingdom within your heart, and hold on to the world loosely so that you are ready when He comes.

Blessings. Have a great day.

Day One Hundred Twenty-Four

Luke 18:1–17

Hello Lucas,

It takes faith to keep praying for something when the answer takes a long time. So Jesus told the story of a wicked judge who answered because he was tired of hearing the same complaint over and over. Then He said, "Will not God bring about justice for his chosen ones, who cry out to him day and night?"

In verses 9–14, He told a story about two men. The first one was a proud, religious man who thought he was better than others. The second one was a "miserable sinner" who humbly repented to God. Jesus said that the only one who went home right with God was the sinner. Why? Because he humbled himself and trusted in God. No one likes a proud person with a condescending, arrogant attitude, and God doesn't either. That's why scripture says, " 'God opposes the proud but shows favor to the humble.' Humble yourselves, therefore, under God's mighty hand, that he may lift you up in due time" (1 Peter 5:5–6).

Then Jesus went on to say that whoever wants to enter the kingdom of God must have childlike faith and humility.

Lucas, Jesus is teaching you this:

1. Keep praying until God answers.
2. Be confident in God's ability to work within you and to clean you.
3. Have childlike faith and stay humble.

Blessings. Have a great day.

Day One Hundred Twenty-Five

Luke 18:18–43

Hello Lucas,

A young man who was a rich official came to Jesus and asked how to have eternal life. Even though the young man had attempted to keep the ten commandments since childhood, Jesus showed him his failure. The young man loved money more than he loved God. Jesus gave him the solution, "Sell everything you have . . . and you will have treasure in heaven. Then come, follow me." The young man went away sad. Imagine that. The Son of God Himself invites you to be His personal disciple, but you turn it down for other things.

In verses 31–33, Jesus described the details of His coming suffering and resurrection. From there He went on to heal a blind man.

Like the rich young ruler, many people try to gain eternal life by following religious laws and church traditions. These things have an appearance of godliness but have no life-changing power. Only a personal encounter with Jesus Christ has the power to bring eternal life.

You have chosen to follow Him, and you have eternal life. Now, His great power is at work changing you from within.

Blessings. Have a great day.

Day One Hundred Twenty-Six

Luke 19:1–27

Hello Lucas,

One of the top tax collectors, being very short, climbed a tree to see Jesus. Noticing his interest, Jesus stopped and spent the day with him. When people insulted Jesus for being with a tax-collecting thief, the man spoke up. He said, "Lord! . . . I give half of my possessions to the poor, and if I have cheated anybody out of anything, I will pay back four times the amount." Jesus openly rewarded the man's humility and repentance by saying, "Today salvation has come to this house." What an amazing difference. A few days earlier, a rich young ruler loved his wealth and lost eternal life. But we see here a wealthy man returning ill-gotten gain in exchange for eternal life.

In verse 11, Jesus went on to explain that all your wealth, resources, and life have been entrusted to you. He expects you to use them faithfully to increase His kingdom. If you are faithful, He will give you more and allow you to rule accordingly in heaven.

Lucas, remember this: You are no fool to give up what you cannot keep in order to gain what you cannot lose.

Blessings. Have a great day.

Day One Hundred Twenty-Seven

Luke 19:28–48

Hello Lucas,

A festive crowd of people usher Jesus toward Jerusalem, singing and praising God for all the miracles they have seen. Approaching the city, while everyone else is rejoicing, Jesus stops and begins to cry. Why? Because those who rejected Him will die in their sins, and the city will be destroyed.

Thirty-seven years later, Emperor Titus decimated Jerusalem.

Notice that Jesus's heart was broken, and He wept openly. Overcome with sorrow for the people, He held nothing back. The world is confused by believing that God is insensitive, unemotional, and harsh. They think He is happy to crush and punish people. The opposite is true. Because justice does demand punishment, He sent Jesus to suffer our punishment for us. In Ezekiel 33:11, He said, "I take no pleasure in the death of the wicked, but rather that they turn from their ways and live."

As a child of your loving heavenly Father, you should also carry that same broken heart for the lost.

Blessings. Have a great day.

Day One Hundred Twenty-Eight

Luke 20:1–20

Hello Lucas,

Jesus was near the temple preaching when the religious leaders challenged His authority. They didn't care that the lame were healed or that the good news was being told. As you talk to others about God, you will experience the same. Some will say, "What makes you an expert on God?" The enemy wants you to stop and be quiet. Just ignore it.

Jesus explained, starting in verse 9. He told a story about workers (the religious leaders) who were hired by the landowner (God) to produce a crop (bring people to God). When the owner sent for the crop, the workers beat the messengers (prophets) and eventually killed the owner's son (Jesus).

The Jewish religious leaders were entrusted to bring people to God. Instead, they used their position for their own advantage. Jesus told them that God would take the field from them and entrust it to faithful people.

God has placed you in His field. You are qualified because He appointed you. Always be ready to bring others to Him, even when challenged.

Blessings. Have a great day.

Day One Hundred Twenty-Nine

Luke 20:21–47

Hello Lucas,

The religious leaders wanted to trap Jesus with trick questions and turn Him over to be crucified so they could maintain their power. Beginning in verse 20, He answered their questions so wisely that they became silent. Many of them did not believe in the resurrection, so beginning in verse 27, Jesus explained that the dead will live again. There is no such thing as reincarnation (our spirit being reborn as another person or animal). There is no second life to live here on earth, no do-overs. After you die, you will stand before God and give an account of yourself. "People are destined to die once, and after that to face judgment" (Hebrews 9 27). "For the trumpet will sound, the dead will be raised imperishable, and we will be changed" (1 Corinthians 15:52).

In verses 41–44, Jesus showed the religious leaders through scriptures that He truly is the Son of God.

Lucas, you have become God's child by faith. When Jesus returns, you will be resurrected, and your frail body will be exchanged for an eternal one like His. That is the future you look forward to.

Blessings. Have a great day.

Day One Hundred Thirty

Luke 21:1–19

Hello Lucas,

Sometimes we feel like we have little to offer God, so we let others, like the talented and wealthy, "help Him." Here, Jesus watched as a widow came and gave only two tiny coins, like pennies. Jesus said, "This poor widow has put in more than all the others." Why? Being poor, that is all she had to live on. From this, you learn that God sees your smallest gift and will honor you for it. Just start by offering what you have to God.

In verse 5, Jesus begins to explain about the end-time events before His return. He tells His followers what they will encounter in the process:

1. Fake Christs will come and try to trick you. (Don't let them deceive you.)
2. Huge wars will come. (Don't be afraid.)
3. You'll be jailed because of my name. (Don't worry. I'll give you words to say.)
4. Family will betray you, and others will hate you, and some of you will die. (Stand firm, and you will have eternal life.)

Your loving heavenly Father has warned you of the trouble to come and has told you how to respond.

Blessings. Have a great day.

Day One Hundred Thirty-One

Luke 21:20–38

Hello Lucas,

God has appointed times and seasons for everything. Nations rise and fall; leaders are appointed and deposed at His command. Man has been given free will, but God, foreknowing our hearts and decisions, has made His plans accordingly. The timeline of earth is set by the clock of heaven.

1. The "Year of the Lord's Favor" began when Christ came to pay for our sins (Luke 4:19).
2. Soon there will be seven years of "Great Trouble" (Matthew 24:21–22; Daniel 9:27).
3. Then Jesus will return to set up God's kingdom on earth for one thousand years (Revelation chapter 20).

Jesus is explaining the "times and seasons" of His return (1 Thessalonians 5:1–4). In verse 34, He tells you to guard your heart so that you are ready for Him. Some believers will not be ready. They will be busy with life's problems, weighed down with self-indulgence and drunkenness, dull of seeing, with no sense of urgency.

Jesus has described these events and God's timeline so that you will be ready for His return. He has told you how to prepare: Be alert, be careful, watch for these events, and pray.

Blessings. Have a great day.

Day One Hundred Thirty-Two

Luke 22:1–38

Hello Lucas,

Jesus celebrated Passover dinner with His disciples. He explained that His broken body and shed blood would cause God's wrath to pass over our sins. John the Baptist foretold this: "Look, the Lamb of God, who takes away the sin of the world!" (John 1:29). Judas left the table, went to the religious leaders, and betrayed Jesus unto death. Psalm 41:9 foretold this event: "Even my close friend, someone I trusted, one who shared my bread, has turned against me." Judas was one of the twelve disciples and worked in the ministry for three years. Notice that Jesus viewed him as "my close friend."

Betrayal of trust by a friend can devastate and cause deep emotional trauma. Jesus did not take it personally. Instead, He saw how God would use Judas's betrayal to bring salvation into the lives of many.

Jesus said you will experience the same. Don't focus on the betrayer and become an emotional mess. Instead, focus on the fact that God knew ahead of time. If you allow Him to use the situation, He will bring good into the lives of many others.

Blessings. Have a great day.

Day One Hundred Thirty-Three

Luke 22:39–53

Hello Lucas,

Jesus had a secret place in an olive grove where He always prayed. He took the disciples there to prepare for His coming suffering. Now we see the source of His strength—prayer and intimate fellowship with God. In verse 47, Judas desecrated that garden sanctuary and betrayed Jesus by handing Him over to an angry mob. Jesus said, "This is your hour—when darkness reigns."

Let's look closer at what happened in His hour of darkness:

1. Jesus was betrayed by a friend.
2. He was in the hands of His enemies.
3. Religious leaders condemned Him.
4. All His followers fled.
5. Peter denied knowing Him.
6. The soldiers mocked and beat Him.

It looked like evil was winning, but God used all of the chaos and darkness to accomplish His own plans.

When it feels like "darkness is reigning" around you, just enter into your secret place of prayer and intimate fellowship with God. Then He will accomplish His own beautiful plans in your life as well.

Blessings. Have a great day.

Day One Hundred Thirty-Four

Luke 22:54–71

Hello Lucas,

The angry mob dragged Jesus before the religious leaders. He was tried and sentenced to death for saying that He was God's Son. For three years, they couldn't get their hands on Him, now He willingly gave Himself up to suffer for our sins.

While Jesus was on trial, Peter denied knowing Him. Earlier, Jesus had said, "Whoever disowns me before others, I will disown before my Father in heaven" (Matthew 10:33). Jesus could have rejected Peter as a coward; instead, He did something different and amazing.

Let's look closer at how Jesus dealt with Peter's failure:
1. Warned him ahead of Satan's plan
2. Told him he would sin by denying Jesus
3. Prayed that he would not fall away
4. Foretold his repentance
5. Gave him a future ministry plan

God knows you intimately. He knows whether you will stand strong or sin. He has not left you alone to wallow in your sins. He is alive within you. He will bring you to the place of strength and maturity.

All you need to do is respond and cooperate when He helps. Let's love Him more and more.

Blessings. Have a great day.

Day One Hundred Thirty-Five

Luke 23:1–25

Hello Lucas,

After convicting Jesus, the religious leaders brought Him before the Roman authorities to get their death sentence approved. They made many false charges, which were baseless and could not be proved. Pilate, the Roman official, pronounced Jesus's innocence and tried three times to release Him. As the mob's chaos escalated, Pilate gave in and handed Jesus over to be crucified.

Here's what Jesus suffered for us:

1. Being flogged with a barbed whip
2. Having a crown of thorns driven into His head
3. Being beaten on His head with sticks
4. Being spit on and having his beard pulled out
5. Being nailed to the cross and speared
6. Experiencing the wrath of God
7. Feeling separated and isolated from God
8. Becoming sin and descending into hell

First Peter 3:18 explains it this way: "Christ also suffered once for sins, the righteous for the unrighteous, to bring you to God." Your sin was transferred to Jesus's account, and He bore the punishment we deserved. He chose to endure the pain because He loves you!

Blessings. Have a great day.

Day One Hundred Thirty-Six

Luke 23:26–43

Hello Lucas,

Is it possible that someone can spend their whole life as a sinner, then be forgiven and saved just two hours before they die? It sounds a lot like Indianna Jones, barely escaping the temple of doom, dodging spears and massive rolling stones with a fortune in his hands.

That is exactly what happened in verse 42. Jesus saved one of the thieves that was being executed beside Him. What did this criminal do that caused Jesus to forgive his sins?

1. He humbled himself.
2. He was the only one to defend Jesus.
3. He openly admitted his sins.
4. He believed that Jesus was King of heaven.
5. He asked Jesus to remember him when He entered His kingdom.

Instantly, Jesus answered his prayer, saying, "Today you will be with me in paradise." If this man was thirty years old, he had lived approximately 262,800 hours and only had two hours left on this earth. That's cutting things real close.

From this you learn that God is full of mercy, compassionate, and abounding in love. He does not want anyone to perish, and it is never too late.

Blessings. Have a great day.

Day One Hundred Thirty-Seven

Luke 23:44–56

Hello Lucas,

Jesus rallied His last strength and in a loud voice committed His Spirit to God. His redemptive work was finished. He successfully removed the things that separated us from God (our sins). At that same moment, God sent an earthquake that removed the temple veil, which separated man from God's presence. Gone is the old system of worship whereby we were distanced from God's holiness. The scripture says, "You who once were far away have been brought near by the blood of Christ" (Ephesians 2:13).

The veil has been torn! Now God invites you to "approach God's throne of grace with confidence, so that we may receive mercy and find grace to help us in our time of need" (Hebrews 4:16).

You now have full access to the glory and presence of your loving heavenly Father. Your body has now become the temple for His Spirit. You can now fellowship with Him anytime and anyplace, wherever you are.

Lucas, boldly enter into a deeper place of daily worship and fellowship with Him.

Blessings. Have a great day.

Day One Hundred Thirty-Eight

Luke 24:1–35

Hello Lucas,

For three years, Jesus ministered powerfully by teaching the people and doing amazing miracles. Most of the people considered Him a prophet and hoped that He was the Messiah who would deliver Israel. Then one day, He was murdered unexpectedly. Most of the people were dazed, confused, and discouraged. Three days later, He rose from the grave and started appearing to His followers. He showed them the scriptures that explained why He had to suffer. It was not to deliver Israel from the Roman oppression but to deliver the world from sin and spiritual bondage.

Humans operate within the here and now, but God operates from an eternal perspective. As His child, the things you encounter have been anticipated by Him for eternal purposes. You must learn to get your eyes off the present situation and ask God, "What is the underlying spiritual issue here?" Once you have His viewpoint, things will make sense and peace will come.

Blessings. Have a great day.

Day One Hundred Thirty-Nine

Luke 24:36–53

Hello Lucas,

Jesus appeared to the whole group of disciples. At first it was hard for them to process. They had mixed emotions of joy, amazement, and disbelief. Their leader, who was disfigured and dead, now stood before them alive. To help them, Jesus showed them His scars and ate with them. He took them through the prophetic scriptures so they could understand these things:

1. Christ would suffer, die, and rise after three days.
2. Repentance and forgiveness of sins would be preached in His name to all nations.
3. They were witnesses to this.
4. He would send the Holy Spirit to help them.

Once they understood, Jesus led them outside Jerusalem, and there He ascended to heaven.

God has chosen the witnessing of that event to save people who are full of sin and headed to hell. It's a simple message: All have sinned. Jesus was punished for their sins. Whoever repents and receives Jesus will be saved.

Blessings. Have a great day.

CHAPTER FIVE

John

Day One Hundred Forty

John 1:1–34

Hello Lucas,

John, moved along by the Holy Spirit, gives one of the most poetic descriptions of Jesus being the "Word of God." In order to fully appreciate the beauty of this, we must ask the question, "What are words?"

Words are merely audible expressions of the contents of a person's heart. Imagine this: A man married a woman, and she did everything perfectly. She cooked amazing meals, kept the house spotless, cleaned his clothes, and even occasionally polished his motorcycle. Then imagine that the first year went by without her speaking a word to him, and that continued for five years. Someone might say, "Wow! He found the perfect wife!" But in reality, if she never spoke, how could he ever discover what was in her heart? What makes her happy or sad? What are her aspirations or dreams? How could he ever know her beautiful personality? That man could never have a truly intimate relationship with her, simply because she never opened her mouth and spoke a word.

God, wanting to share all of His thoughts and love for you, sent His Son to tell you all that was in His heart. Jesus says later in the book of John, "I do nothing on my own but speak just what the Father has taught me" (John 8:28).

John also says this about Jesus: "He was with God in the beginning. Through him all things were made." He is God, the Word of God, the light of the world, full of grace and truth, and God's one and only Son.

The Bible is a compilation of God's love letters to you. Read them every day so that you can truly know His heart for you.

Blessings. Have a great day.

Day One Hundred Forty-One

John 1:35–51

Hello Lucas,

John the Baptist testified to everyone that Jesus was the Son of God. When two of his disciples heard this, they left John the Baptist and followed Jesus (the apostles John and Andrew). Jesus went on to call Peter, Phillip, and Nathaniel (who was also called Bartholomew) to follow Him.

I find Nathaniel's story interesting. His friend Phillip told him about Jesus. At first, he was actually skeptical, until he met Jesus personally. What changed Nathaniel's mind? Jesus shared all kinds of personal things about Nathaniel that a normal person wouldn't know, so he was convinced and became one of the twelve disciples. Tradition says that he became a missionary to India and Armenia, then died as a martyr.

From this, we see that even though people may not believe in Jesus, He is thinking about them. He knows them and has a plan for their lives. Like Phillip, you just need to introduce others to Jesus. Then they can experience for themselves and believe.

Blessings. Have a great day.

Day One Hundred Forty-Two

John 2:1–11

Hello Lucas,

Jesus attended a large wedding celebration with His mother and disciples. When the wine ran out, His mother asked for His help, so He turned 180 gallons of water into fine wine. This was His first public miracle. Jesus did not just meet the need but made "the best" wine. Because of this miracle, His disciples put their faith in Him.

Jesus later said, "Whoever believes in me will do the works I have been doing, and they will do even greater things than these, because I am going to the Father" (John 14:12).

As a follower of Christ, you must also realize that the problems around you are opportunities for miracles. You do not have to worry about how or if a miracle will happen; you just need to pray. When someone shares a need, don't tell them you will pray later. Stop what you are doing and pray with them at that moment. God wants to answer so that people will put their faith in Jesus. You may be the bridge that brings them "the best" thing that they have ever experienced.

Blessings. Have a great day.

Day One Hundred Forty-Three

John 2:12–25

Hello Lucas,

Jesus and His disciples went to the temple courtyard where tables were set up for exchanging money and for the selling of religious items. This might seem innocent enough, but make no mistake, the market was there to make money and take advantage of people. Jesus knew this and cleaned house by turning tables over and chasing off the merchants. One thousand years earlier, King David prophesied this event, saying, "Zeal for your house consumes me" (Psalm 69:9).

Like the people of Jesus's time, there are people today who include God into their lives for personal gain. They don't want to know Him; they only want to know what He will do for them. The Bible says, "Don't you know that you yourselves are God's temple and that God's Spirit dwells in your midst?" (1 Corinthians 3:16).

Lucas, keep the temple of your heart free from greed. Pursue a personal relationship with God first, then the other blessings will follow.

Blessings. Have a great day.

Day One Hundred Forty-Four

John 3:1–21

Hello Lucas,

One of the religious leaders secretly came to Jesus at night. Jesus told him directly, "No one can see the kingdom of God unless they are born again." Then He explained that our parents first gave birth to our flesh, but man's spirit must be reborn by God's Spirit.

Jesus went on to say that God sent Him to bring the light and save the world, not to condemn it, and that the people who love their sins and darkness are already condemned because they will not receive Him.

From this you see that being a religious person, joining a religious group, or doing religious duties does not save or change you. Instead, you must put your faith in Jesus and allow God's Spirit to come in and change your spirit from the inside out.

Lucas, continue to stand in the spiritual light so that your sins can be revealed, and let the Holy Spirit begin the remodel project. Then you will be truly born of the Spirit.

Blessings. Have a great day.

Day One Hundred Forty-Five

John 3:22–36

Hello Lucas,

As Jesus's ministry grew and John the Baptist's declined, John responded by saying: "He must become greater; I must become less." Notice that he considered himself to be nothing more than a road sign, pointing all eyes to Jesus.

John gave witness to the truth about Jesus. What did John tell the people about Him?

1. He loves you like the groom loves the bride.
2. He came from above and is above all.
3. He tells what He has seen in heaven.
4. He speaks the words of God.
5. He was given all authority from God.
6. Whoever believes in Him has life.
7. God's wrath is on all who reject Him.

Crowds of thousands turned to Jesus because of John's response. There is great power in that kind of humility. When people look at you, do they see Jesus, or is life all about you? Let there be more of Him and less of you. Become a humble "road sign" so that all eyes are on Him. Then people can find their loving Savior.

Blessings. Have a great day.

Day One Hundred Forty-Six

John 4:1–30

Hello Lucas,

As Jesus went about preaching, He stopped at a well and asked a woman for a drink, then offered her "living water" that would cure her thirst. Confused, she asked what He meant. In order to show that she had deep emotional and spiritual thirst, He said, "You have had five husbands, and the man you now have is not your husband." Because He knew personal things about her and He spoke so clearly about God, she wondered if He might be the promised Messiah. He told her, "I am."

This woman had inner thirsts that human relationships could not satisfy. The "living water" that Jesus offered her was the Holy Spirit. He said, "[It] will become . . . a spring of water welling up to eternal life." She was so happy, and she left her water jug, ran into town, and compelled everyone to come see Jesus!

Like this woman, people are trying to fill their thirsty hearts with things that cannot satisfy: relationships, drugs, riches, careers, hobbies, and so on.

Lucas, point the thirsty ones you meet to Jesus so that they can drink His living water and thirst no more.

Blessings. Have a great day.

Day One Hundred Forty-Seven

John 4:31–54

Hello Lucas,

Jesus's disciples met Him at the well and offered Him lunch. Instead, He turned their attention to spiritual food. He explained that finishing God's work of "harvesting" people for eternal life was His food. Have you ever been so focused on something or so excited that eating didn't interest you? That's how Jesus felt. He knew that the people there were ready to come to God. If He waited, the opportunity and harvest would be lost.

In verse 40, after hearing this woman speak, the people of that area urged Jesus to stay and share with them also. Because of her story and because of Jesus's words, many people believed in Him.

Years ago, I led an o d man to Jesus. The next day, I heard that he died. Because I stopped mowing my lawn and took time to visit with him, his soul was "harvested" to eternal life. If I would have put him off, he would have died in his sins. If you are aware of the harvest around you and pay attention, you will avoid a spiritual crop failure. Many will come up and thank you when you meet them in heaven.

Blessings. Have a great day.

Day One Hundred Forty-Eight

John 5:1–30

Hello Lucas,

Jesus attended a religious festival in Jerusalem and healed a man who had been paralyzed for thirty-five years. The religious leaders ignored the amazing miracle and persecuted Jesus because this "work" was done on a holy day. So He said, "My Father is always at his work" and "What the Father does the Son also does."

Jesus explained that because He, God's Son, came and lived as a man, God gave Him authority to do these things:

1. Raise men to life on the last day.
2. Judge their works on the last day.
3. Give eternal life to those who believe His words.

The religious leaders were furious because Jesus called Himself God's Son. They had the Word of God that said God would send His Son, but their hearts had strayed so far, they could not see it. Instead, they tried to destroy the promised blessing that God had sent them, His Son.

Today, some people still try to destroy their blessing, but God is patiently at work revealing Jesus to them.

Blessings. Have a great day.

Day One Hundred Forty-Nine

John 5:31–47

Hello Lucas,

The religious leaders refused to believe that Jesus was God's Son, so He showed them how they missed it. He listed three things that gave witness to this truth.

1. John the Baptist said it was true.
2. The healing miracles proved it.
3. God foretold it in the scriptures.

Jesus went on to correct them for not knowing the Word of God and not receiving Him. They claimed to trust in Moses and the law, so He said that Moses himself would accuse them because "he wrote about Me."

Moses had prophesied: "I will raise up for them a prophet like you from among their fellow sraelites, and I will put my words in his mouth. He will tell them everything I command him. . . . You must listen to him" (Deuteronomy 18:18, 15).

God has been faithful to provide all the evidence needed to see that Jesus is His Son. Whoever accepts Him and His words will have eternal life.

Blessings. Have a great day.

Day One Hundred Fifty

John 6:1–27

Hello Lucas,

John confirms that Jesus lived a life filled with miracles. Thousands followed Him because of the excitement of the moment and what they could get out of it (physical healing, food, entertainment, hanging out with the crowd, being a part of an exciting movement). Jesus kept pointing their attention away from this temporary world toward heaven and eternal life.

Again, the crowds were hungry, so Jesus fed five thousand with a boy's lunch. When He left and walked across the sea by night, the people noticed that He did not go in a boat. In the morning, they crossed the sea and found Him. Jesus knew their hearts and told them directly, "You are looking for me . . . because you ate the loaves and had your fill."

As a follower of Jesus, you must not merely seek what you can get from God's hand here on earth. You must set your heart on the things above because that is where your true eternal future lies.

Blessings. Have a great day.

Day One Hundred Fifty-One

John 6:28–71

Hello Lucas,

When Jesus fed five thousand with five loaves of bread and two fish, the crowds focused only on the food. So in verses 35 and 51, Jesus declared, "I am the bread of life. . . . This bread is my flesh, which I will give for the life of the world." Most of the crowd could not catch the spiritual meaning, because they were not hungry for God. So they left offended, saying, "How can this man give us his flesh to eat?"

Then Jesus told the remaining followers clearly, "The Spirit gives life; the flesh counts for nothing. The words I have spoken to you—they are full of the Spirit and life." Jesus was speaking about spiritual food and that He would offer His body as a sacrifice for the sins of the world.

In what way was Jesus the bread of heaven? He spoke the words—the "bread" of God. He offered His body as "bread" to be broken for us.

Lucas, you may ask, "How do I eat this heavenly bread?" By faith and obedience. Believe and obey His words. Accept by faith His broken-body suffering for you. That's why we take communion, to remember that His body was broken for our healing and His blood was poured out for the remission of our sins.

Blessings. Have a great day.

Day One Hundred Fifty-Two

John 7:1–24

Hello Lucas,

Jesus came into the world to bring the words of truth from God. He did not speak His own words or seek His own honor. There is such a thing as absolute truth and the sometimes-painful reality that follows. So it is said, "The truth hurts."

The religious leaders wanted to kill Jesus because of the truth that He spoke. His own brothers did not believe until He was resurrected, and so they insulted Him. In verse 7, Jesus said, "The world . . . hates me because I testify that its works are evil."

The people of this world present themselves as intelligent, pure, and truth-seeking. But in reality, any revelation that does not support their self-indulgent lifestyle is rejected by them.

As you speak the truth of God, you will be called things like *radical*, *Nazi*, and *terrorist*, and your message will be labeled "hate speech." So why should you speak at all? Jesus said, "You will know the truth, and the truth will set you free" (John 8:32). There is only one path to spiritual freedom, and that is knowing the truth, and Jesus is the truth. As you continue to speak the truth, the humble will accept it and gain life.

Blessings. Have a great day.

Day One Hundred Fifty-Three

John 7:25–53

Hello Lucas,

Jesus spent three years speaking the Word of God and showing the Jews how their own prophets confirmed all that He said and did. God had prophesied that Jesus would come by way of Galilee; it is very clear. "In the future [God] will honor Galilee of the nations, by the Way of the Sea, beyond Jordan" (Isaiah 9:1). But the religious leaders, opposing Jesus, said, "Look into [the scriptures], and you will find that a prophet does not come out of Galilee" (verse 52). The Jews rejected Jesus's words and refused to acknowledge their own scriptures.

You may say, "If I were there, I would not have done that. I would have listened to Jesus." Let me ask you a question: Are you so sure? Today, many people profess to be Christians and hope to go to heaven. But they don't want to read their Bible or listen to a sermon. Days, weeks, and years go by without any interest in hearing or doing Jesus's words.

That type of Christian has already rejected the teachings of Jesus and is no better off than the religious leaders of Jesus's day.

Lucas, continue to read and receive the Word of God. Even the difficult teachings.

Blessings. Have a great day.

Day One Hundred Fifty-Four

John 8:1–11

Hello Lucas,

The religious leaders, still wanting to trap and accuse Jesus, brought to Him a woman caught in adultery. Under the law of Moses, she deserved death. If Jesus said otherwise, they could seize Him. So He agreed to her execution with one stipulation: The first stone was to be cast by a person who was without sin. Being conscience-stricken, her accusers left. Jesus did not come into this world to execute judgment; He came to save people from their sins. So He said to the woman, "Neither do I condemn you. . . Go now and leave your life of sin."

Sin eventually brings people to the brink of physical and spiritual death. It is there, in that desperate condition, that Jesus offers an undeserved pardon. In doing so, He is not condoning the lifestyle of sin and death. Instead, He is offering a new culture of life, one filled with forgiveness, freedom, and purity. He has made a way out of sin and provided a newfound freedom. So He says, "Go now and leave your life of sin."

Lucas, the angel told Mary, "And you are to give him the name Jesus [Jehovah is salvation], because he will save his people from their sins" (Matthew 1:21). Notice the scripture does not say, "He shall be called *forgiver*." It says *Savior*. Jesus did not only come to forgive you but to save you from all of the bondage and power of sin so that you can live a life of total freedom!

Blessings. Have a great day.

Day One Hundred Fifty-Five

John 8:12–59

Hello Lucas,

God had promised the Jews that He would send the Messiah, but they were expecting a political leader, not a spiritual savior. He spoke spiritual truth, and they were only thinking in earthly concepts. Their hearts were hard, so they could not grasp what He said. Over and over again, He explained who He was and what God was trying to say to them.

John tells us that Jesus described Himself as "I am" forty-five times. This was a phrase known to the Jews. When God revealed Himself to Moses, He only described Himself as "I am that I am."

Jesus said, "I am"

the light of the world,
the bread of life,
the way and the truth and the life,
the resurrection and the life,
the only door,
the good shepherd,
the true vine,
the Messiah
from above, not of this world, and
the Son of God and King of the Jews.

Jesus told them, "If you do not believe that I am [the one I claim to be], you will indeed die in your sins."

Lucas, however, you do know and believe in Him.

Blessings. Have a great day.

Day One Hundred Fifty-Six

John 9:1–12

Hello Lucas,

Jesus was in the spotlight because of His powerful miracles and amazing teaching. The people were always questioning who He was. They couldn't figure out who His father was or where He came from. When He told them that God was His father, they tried to stone Him. Jesus escaped and immediately healed a blind man. Then Jesus said something amazing about the man. "This happened so that the works of God might be displayed in him."

Let's look closer:

1. The man was born blind and lived that way for at least thirty years.
2. God created him blind for this moment and purpose in history.
3. When he was healed, the people could see that Jesus was God's Son.

Lucas, it is most important that you understand that your birth was not just a by-product of your mother and father coming together. God planned your creation and destined you to be born in this very generation for a purpose. You may not always understand the things that life deals you, but if you trust in God and let His work be displayed through your life, He will work all things for the good—both for you and those around you.

Blessings. Have a great day.

Day One Hundred Fifty-Seven

John 9:13–41

Hello Lucas,

The religious leaders investigated the healing of the blind man and learned from his parents that he was born blind. After telling his own story, the man said, "If [Jesus] were not from God, he could do nothing." The leaders had already agreed whoever said Jesus was Christ would be expelled from the temple. So they insulted the man and threw him out.

This man, his family, and their neighbors gave testimony to the truth that the man was blind, and now Jesus had healed him, but the rulers rejected the truth. They were upset that Jesus healed on a holy day and called Him a sinner. Jesus had shown them earlier that it was lawful to do good on the Sabbath, explaining that they themselves help their own animals out of the ditch on the Sabbath.

The man who was once blind could now see that Jesus was the Christ. The religious leaders who claimed to see, were spiritually blind and rejected their Savior. "Amazing grace, how sweet the sound that saved a wretch like me; I once was lost, but now I'm found, was blind but now I see."

Blessings. Have a great day.

Day One Hundred Fifty-Eight

John 10:1–21

Hello Lucas,

Jesus said, "Very truly I tell you, I am the gate for the sheep. All who have come before me are thieves and robbers. . . . whoever enters through me will be saved." In saying this, Jesus declared that He was the only way to eternal life. All who came before and after Him—Buddha, Confucius, Hinduism, Mohammed, etc.—are not the way. The world says, "All religions lead to eternal life, and to say otherwise is bias of you."

Consider this comparison: You go to the bus station and there are ten buses. Nine are broken down, and only one is working. There is nothing arrogant or bias about you saying, "There is only one way to my destination. The working bus is the only way!"

When God created the earth, He knew that man would sin, and He made a plan to save you. The death and resurrection of Jesus was that plan from the beginning. Jesus said, "I am the way and the truth and the life. No one comes to the Father except through me." This is not bias or intolerance of others; it is simply the truth.

Blessings. Have a great day.

Day One Hundred Fifty-Nine

John 10:22–42

Hello Lucas,

Jesus had clearly told the Jews that He was the Christ and that the miracles done in His Father's name proved it. He said, "You do not believe because you are not my sheep." They wanted to stone Him for saying that He was God's Son and that He was one with God. Their hearts were hard and full of evil, so they could not receive the truth.

Jesus said this about His "sheep":

1. I know them.
2. They hear my voice.
3. I give them eternal life.
4. They shall never perish.
5. No one can take them from me.
6. My Father gave them to me.

Jesus is the Good Shepherd sent from the heavenly Father. You have believed and, by faith, belong to Him. All of His protection and promises belong to you. "But for those who are self-seeking and who reject the truth and follow evil, there will be wrath and anger" (Romans 2:8). Why? Because they love the evil that they do, and they reject the truth.

Blessings. Have a great day.

Day One Hundred Sixty

John 11:1–37

Hello Lucas,

One of Jesus's friends named Lazarus was sick unto death. When asked to come and heal him, Jesus intentionally delayed, and the man died. Jesus told His disciples, "For your sake I am glad I was not there, so that you may believe." He had already told them, "This sickness will not end in death."

When Jesus arrived, the family had been mourning for four days. Then Lazarus's sisters told Jesus, "If you had been here, [he] would not have died." Then Jesus replied, "I am the resurrection and the life. The one who believes in me will live, even though they die."

Why didn't Jesus go earlier and heal Lazarus before he died? It was God's plan to show the people that Jesus was the Christ, the Son of God. If Jesus could bring Lazarus back to life in front of everyone, multitudes would give glory to God and put their faith in Jesus.

Jesus promised you that He will return to earth and set up His kingdom, and on that "last day," He will raise you to life. This story shows you that He is God's Son and that He will do what He promised. Just joyfully wait for His return!

Blessings. Have a great day.

Day One Hundred Sixty-One

John 11:38–57

Hello Lucas,

Four days dead and without hope, Lazarus lay in a cave-tomb sealed with a stone over its entrance. When Jesus arrived, He asked that the stone be rolled back.

Martha, Lazarus's sister, said, "By this time there is a bad odor."

Jesus replied, "If you believe, you will see the glory of God." Jesus yelled, "Lazarus, come out!" And he came out still wrapped in his burial cloth. Because of this miracle, many put their faith in Jesus.

God wants to interrupt people's lives, show His glory, and reveal His Son so that they can have eternal life. Often, He has to do something dramatic to get their attention, then they realize that "only God could do this."

Lucas, maybe you are experiencing a situation where things in your life are like Lazarus: four days dead, already buried, and stinking terribly with zero chance of hope. If you encounter that situation, take courage. you serve a miracle-working God who gives life to dead situations. "If you believe, you will see the glory of God."

Blessings. Have a great day.

Day One Hundred Sixty-Two

John 12:1–26

Hello Lucas,

By raising a man from the dead, Jesus proved that He was God's Son. Instead of accepting that truth, the religious leaders conspired to destroy the evidence by killing both Jesus and Lazarus.

However, large crowds believed. They gathered together around Jesus as He rode a young donkey into Jerusalem. The people wanted to install Jesus as King of the Jews. Instead, He said, "Unless a kernel of wheat falls to the ground and dies," it can't produce fruit. In saying this, He showed that He would not become an earthly king at that time but give up His life so that many could have eternal life. Jesus went on to explain that we should serve God's eternal plans instead of our earthly agendas, and promised, "My Father will honor the one who serves me."

Like Jesus, you have learned that you must die to earthly ambitions and selfish desires. Continue to discover and live God's plans and purposes for your life. Only then can you bring forth much fruit unto eternal life.

Blessings. Have a great day.

Day One Hundred Sixty-Three

John 12:27–50

Hello Lucas,

In a few days, Jesus will be crucified, so He spoke openly about His destiny:

1. It was for this reason (death and resurrection) that I came to this hour.
2. If I be lifted up from the earth (on the cross), I will draw all men unto me.
3. Now the prince of this world (Satan and his authority) will be driven out.

Many of the religious leaders came to believe in Jesus, but they would not openly confess their faith. Why? They were afraid of losing their position of honor and the respect that people showed them. Jesus reminded them that He only spoke God's words, so to reject Him was to reject God who sent Him.

In the kingdom of God, there are no "secret" believers. If you truly believe in Jesus, you will eventually confess that faith openly, regardless of the cost. The reward will be eternal life.

Blessings. Have a great day.

Day One Hundred Sixty-Four

John 13:1–17

Hello Lucas,

When the evening Passover meal was served, Jesus picked up a servant's towel and proceeded to wash His disciples' feet. After doing so, He explained, "Now that I, your Lord and Teacher, have washed your feet, you also should wash one another's feet." Although Jesus was both King and Lord, He expressed His love through a lifestyle of servanthood. This humility brought many into the kingdom of God. He is asking you to have that same kind of attitude. How then do you "wash the feet" of other Christians?

1. Develop a humble, helpful attitude.
2. Do not think that you are greater than others.
3. Look for ways to help others grow in their walk with the Lord.
4. Walking through life can be messy; help wash the mess off their lives.

John described it this way: "[Jesus] loved them to the end" by doing this.

Lucas, follow Jesus's example and show your brothers and sisters the full extent of your love by taking up a lifestyle of servanthood.

Blessings. Have a great day.

Day One Hundred Sixty-Five

John 13:18–38

Hello Lucas,

During the last supper, Jesus told His disciples that one of them would betray Him. "I am te ling you now before it happens, so that when it does happen you will believe that I am who I am." From this we see that God knows all and is in control.

Because of His great love for the world, Jesus was about to enter the distress of suffering and death. Jesus commanded His disciples to walk in that same love. In verse 34–35, He said, "A new command I give you: Love one another. As I have loved you, so you must love one another. By this everyone will know that you are my disciples, if you love one another."

Jesus expressed His love by giving up His life for you. If that single act of love provided forgiveness for the whole world, your generation may change if you do likewise. God is love, and when you love, the world sees that you are a child of God. Since you have entered His family, continue to express that same devotion to your brothers and sisters. There is great power when you walk in love.

Blessings. Have a great day.

Day One Hundred Sixty-Six

John 14:1–14

Hello Lucas,

In a few hours, Jesus will be betrayed, suffer, and die. He took much time to explain everything to His disciples so that they would be prepared. Let's look at what He said:

1. Don't let your hearts be troubled.
2. You trust God; trust me too.
3. I am returning to my Father.
4. I am preparing a place for you there.
5. I will come back and get you.
6. I am the way to the Father.
7. No one comes to the Father except through me.

Then He explained His relationship with God. "I am in the Father, and . . . the Father is in me. The words I say to you I do not speak on my own authority. Rather, it is the Father, living in me, who is doing his work." Then He added, "Whoever believes in me will do the works I have been doing, and they will do even greater things than these, because I am going to the Father."

Jesus is preparing a place for you in heaven, and He will return for you. Until then, Jesus has empowered you to do good works and miracles so that others may find their way to God. He is the way.

Blessings. Have a great day.

Day One Hundred Sixty-Seven

John 14:15–31

Hello Lucas,

Jesus continued to prepare His disciples for His departure. In verse 18, He said, "I will not leave you as orphans." He promised to send a helper, the Spirit of Truth, to help those who love and obey Him.

As a newborn child, you have come into God's family with a lot of mess from your old life. Jesus has not left you like an orphan to deal with this alone. He sent His Holy Spirit, who will "teach you all things." He will help you unpack all of your "baggage" and deal with it properly.

In verse 21, Jesus went on to challenge your sincerity by saying, "Whoever has my commands and keeps them is the one who loves me. [He] will be loved by my Father, and I too will love them and show myself to them."

Your loving heavenly Father has sent an amazing helper who will help you grow up to become like Him. Show your sincerity by loving and obeying Him.

Blessings. Have a great day.

Day One Hundred Sixty-Eight

John 15:1–17

Hello Lucas,

Jesus told a parable to His disciples showing the importance of staying connected with Him. In this "picture story," God is the gardener, Jesus is the main vine, and we are branches that grow fruit. Jesus explained it this way:

1. I have chosen you to bear much spiritual fruit that will last.
2. You cannot bear fruit by yourself.
3. Stay attached to me to bear fruit.
4. Stay attached or you will die.
5. God cuts off unproductive branches.
6. Dead branches are taken and burned.
7. God prunes productive branches so they will produce more fruit.

Then He told how to stay connected:

1. Let His words remain in you.
2. Remain in His love by obeying Him.
3. Love each other as He loved you.

You are His branch and must receive sap from the main vine in order to live. Every day you must connect with Jesus by reading and doing His words and by loving others. If you disconnect from these things, you will quickly dry up and die. Stay connected and bear fruit.

Blessings. Have a great day.

Day One Hundred Sixty-Nine

John 15:18–27

Hello Lucas,

The inhabitants and systems of this world are flawed and fail to recognize the evil spiritual forces that influence them. Jesus came to make us aware and save us.

He warned His disciples:

1. I have chosen you out of the world and you do not belong to it.
2. The world hated and persecuted me and will do the same to you.
3. The world does not know God and will treat you bad because of my name.

Jesus told you these things ahead so that you would not be surprised, get discouraged, and leave Him. Once, you were moved along by sin and evil. You were a part of the fallen world system. But God in His great mercy called you out, cleansed you, and gave you a new heart.

Now that you are a Christian, do not be surprised if people treat you bad. It is not you that they hate. They are rejecting God's goodness in you because they are still part of the fallen world system.

Blessings. Have a great day.

Day One Hundred Seventy

John 16:1–18

Hello Lucas,

Soon, Jesus would be arrested, so He told His disciples, "It is for your good that I am going away. Unless I go away, the Advocate will not come to you; but if I go, I will send him to you." What did He mean? While on earth, Jesus's ability to minister was limited by His physical body. But when the Holy Spirit came, He would be able to do unlimited work within the hearts of everyone, everywhere. All around the world, the Holy Spirit is now at work, convincing people to believe in Jesus. He is convicting them about their sin, teaching them to be righteous, and pronouncing judgments against the fallen prince of this world (Satan).

The Holy Spirit is also at work within your life. Jesus promised, "When he, the Spirit of truth, comes, he will guide you into all the truth." Open your life to this precious helper. Let Him lead and guide you and fill you with all truth. When you read the Bible, ask Him to help you understand and to lead your reading. Then you can receive all that your heavenly Father has for your spiritual well-being.

Blessings. Have a great day.

Day One Hundred Seventy-One

John 16:19–33

Hello Lucas,

Jesus knew that His disciples would soon experience confusion and grief because of His crucifixion and death. Accomplishing anything of value always comes at a great cost. So in verse 21, He told them, "A woman giving birth to a child has pain because her time has come; but when her baby is born she forgets the anguish." He told them, "Now is your time of grief, but I will see you again and you will rejoice, and no one will take away your joy."

Now that you are Jesus's disciple, it's your turn to serve in His kingdom. As He works through you accomplishing great things, you will also experience times of great suffering. In verse 33, He said: "In this world you will have trouble. But take heart! I have overcome the world."

Remember, your present sufferings are small and won't last very long, but they will produce eternal blessings that will last forever!

Blessings. Have a great day.

Day One Hundred Seventy-Two

John 17:1–19

Hello Lucas,

Jesus spent His final, few hours of freedom praying for Himself and His disciples. Out of His great concern for them, He prayed for His followers: "I protected them and kept them safe by that name you gave me. . . . I will remain in the world no longer, but they are still in the world, and I am coming to you. Holy Father, protect them by the power of *your name, the name you gave me*."

He also prayed these things:

1. Protect them from the evil one.
2. Don't take them out of the world.
3. Keep them clean and separate from the world by your Word of truth.
4. I am sending them into the world (to speak God's Word and tell of Jesus).
5. May they be full of my joy.
6. May they be one as we are one.

Facing death, the care of Jesus's followers was foremost on His mind. He knew the power of prayer and entrusted your safe keeping to the heavenly Father. As a follower of Jesus, you should not worry. You may be in the world, but you are not subject to it. You are under the prayer covering of Jesus and safeguarded by God. Hallelujah!

Blessings. Have a great day.

Day One Hundred Seventy-Three

John 17:20–26

Hello Lucas,

After preparing and praying for His disciples, Jesus prayed for you! This is what He said in verse 20: "My prayer is not for [the disciples] alone. I pray also for those who will believe in me through their message." Here are the things that Jesus prayed for you:

1. That you would be one with other Christians (one in Spirit, in the bond of love, and in complete unity) just like God and Jesus are one.
2. That He, Jesus, would live in you just as God lives in Jesus.
3. That you may live with Jesus in heaven.

Jesus did not stop praying for you two thousand years ago. Scripture tells us that we have a great high priest, Jesus the Son of God, who knows your weaknesses (Hebrews 4:14–16) and who is at the right hand of God interceding (praying) for you (Romans 8:34).

Lucas, you have accepted Jesus, and He has not left you to struggle alone. He completely understands every intimate detail of your life and personality. Every day, He, like the perfect lawyer, is representing you before the Father. Because of this, God is busy doing a good work within your heart and life.

Blessings. Have a great day.

Day One Hundred Seventy-Four

John 18:1–27

Hello Lucas,

As soon as Jesus finished praying, Judas the betrayer came, leading a detachment of soldiers and religious officials who arrested Jesus. When Peter saw this, he took his sword and started swinging, but Jesus stopped him and said, "Shall I not drink the cup the Father has given me?" Then all the disciples ran away, and Jesus was bound and taken away.

From this we see that God had a plan: Jesus would suffer and die for our sins, then raise to life. How did God's people react to that plan?

1. Jesus embraced the plan and drank of the cup of suffering.
2. Judas wanted to profit from the plan, so he sold Jesus out for money.
3. Peter wanted to control the plan himself, so he took up the sword.
4. The rest of the disciples were so shocked about the plan, they ran off.

You are one of God's people, and He wants to accomplish His plans through you. How will you react to that plan? May you always have the grace to embrace it.

Blessings. Have a great day.

Day One Hundred Seventy-Five

John 18:28–40

Hello Lucas,

Around seven hundred years earlier, Isaiah prophesied the exact details of Jesus's arrest, saying, "By oppression and judgment he was taken away" (Isaiah 53:8). So about 2 a.m., Jesus was arrested and put through several mock trials. At that time, all of the disciples fled for fear. John and Peter observed the trial from a distance. When people recognized Peter, he denied knowing Jesus three separate times. He left that place and wept bitterly because of his failure. Earlier, Jesus had told him, "Before the rooster crows, you will disown me three times!" (John 13:38). God knows all things ahead of time.

With this knowledge, Jesus prepared Peter for his failure by

1. praying for him ahead,
2. telling him he would fail,
3. telling him to pray for himself, and
4. restoring him after the failure.

God knows and orchestrates world events; He also knows you better than you know yourself. You are His child, and He will care for you, just as He did for Peter. Rest in His faithfulness and always be ready to repent.

Blessings. Have a great day.

Day One Hundred Seventy-Six

John 19:1–16

Hello Lucas,

Jesus testified that He was the Son of God and the King of heaven. The Jews who had brought Jesus to stand trial before Pilot stated, "We have a law, and according to that law he must die, because he claimed to be the Son of God." Pilate deemed Jesus innocent and attempted to release Him. When the Jews stirred up the crowds, Pilate caved in and handed Him over to be Crucified. When Jesus spoke the truth, the Jews wanted to kill Him. When Pilate heard the truth, he listened but lacked the back-bone to stand up for it.

When God presents a truth to you, it may challenge your current belief and may not be what you want to hear. Accepting that truth may require a change that costs you a lot. I have met Christians who refuse to respond to truth once they find it in the Bible. According to Jesus, if you are on His side, you will listen to truth and act appropriately. If your lifestyle or tradition is not based upon God's Word, you must change.

Blessings. Have a great day.

Day One Hundred Seventy-Seven

John 19:17–42

Hello Lucas,

John was an eyewitness to the crucifixion of Jesus and left this written testimony:

1. He was crucified on Golgotha hill.
2. Pilate put a notice on the cross declaring Jesus as "King of the Jews."
3. The soldiers divided His clothes.
4. He suffered thirst.
5. The soldiers did not break His legs.
6. His side was pierced with a spear.
7. He said, "It is finished," then died.

John emphasized that he saw this and "his testimony is true," and he testifies so that you may believe that "these things happened so that the scripture would be fulfilled." Here is one of the prophetic scriptures he was referring to: "They pierce my hands and my feet. . . . They divide my clothes among them and cast lots for my garment" (Psalm 22:16–18).

Joseph of Arimathea and Nicodemus took Jesus's body and prepared it for burial using seventy-five pounds of spices and linen, then they placed Him in a tomb.

Notice, these two men were "secret disciples" while Jesus was alive. But when they saw Him openly suffer public humiliation and death, they became brave. They openly collected and cared for the body of their Savior.

Lucas, follow their example of open, unashamed love and devotion to Jesus.

Blessings. Have a great day.

Day One Hundred Seventy-Eight

John 20:1–18

Hello Lucas,

When Jesus rose from the grave, He first appeared to Mary Magdalene. Let's look closer at her life:

1. Jesus had cast seven demons from her.
2. She followed along with the disciples, learning as He taught.
3. She regularly provided finances for the ministry.
4. She stayed and witnessed His crucifixion and death.
5. She came to help with His burial.
6. She was the first one to see Him raised from the dead.

Jesus had already chosen twelve men to be witnesses of His life, death, and resurrection to the world. But from this account, we also see that God does not show sexism. Jesus showed Himself alive to a woman first and told her to go tell the disciples that He had risen. Scripture tells us that "There is neither Jew nor Gentile, neither slave nor free, nor is there male and female, for you are all one in Christ Jesus" (Galatians 3:28).

You are a child of God, no longer separated by nationality, age, gender, or social class. Like Mary Magdalene, God will use you to do great things for His kingdom, if you are willing.

Blessings. Have a great day.

Day One Hundred Seventy-Nine

John 20:19–31

Hello Lucas,

Jesus rose in the morning, but the disciples didn't grasp it until that night. They were afraid for their lives and were staying behind locked doors. Then Jesus appeared in the room, showing Himself alive. When Thomas arrived later, the others told him that Jesus was alive. This seemed too incredible, so he said, "Unless I see the nail marks in his hands and put my finger where the nails were, and put my hand into his side, I will not believe." A week later, they were all together when Jesus appeared again. He showed His hands and side to Thomas and said, "Stop doubting and believe. . . . Because you have seen me, you have believed; blessed are those who have not seen and yet have believed." John went on to say that he recorded these things so that we will believe that Jesus is the Christ, the Son of God, and have eternal life in His name.

Even though you have not seen Jesus yet, you have believed because of their testimony. When you believe God, it pleases Him and brings eternal blessings into your life.

Blessings. Have a great day.

Day One Hundred Eighty

John 21:1–14

Hello Lucas,

After His resurrection, Jesus had not yet given His disciples their next direction, so most of them followed Peter to the sea of Galilee and went fishing. There they spent the night catching nothing. Someone on the shore called out, "Throw your net on the right side of the boat," and when they did, it overflowed with fish. Realizing that it was Jesus, they went ashore and were surprised to count 153 large fish, yet the net was undamaged.

Notice how these same events happened when Jesus first called them to follow Him. For three years they had direction and purpose ministering with Him, but all of that was taken away when Jesus was crucified. Now, Jesus is bringing their attention back to their original calling: "I will send you out to fish for people."

After coming to Jesus, you may encounter setbacks that make you lose your sense of direction and commitment. Rest assured, He will call you back to that first love and rebuild direction and confidence in your life.

Blessings. Have a great day.

Day One Hundred Eighty-One

John 21:15–25

Hello Lucas,

As you see, Jesus was waiting for the disciples on the beach and had prepared bread and fish on a fire. This was the third time that He appeared to them. After eating, Jesus asked Peter the same question three times in a row: "Do you love me more than these (fish and fishing)?" Peter was broken and said, "Yes, Lord, you know that I love you." Then Jesus replied, "Feed my sheep."

Let's look closer:

1. When Jesus was on trial, Peter lied and denied knowing Him three times.
2. Now, instead of telling Peter that he was a miserable failure, Jesus gave him an opportunity to reconcile the failure and reaffirm his love.
3. Then He gave Peter direction and purpose for his life. He was to catch men for the kingdom of heaven and feed them God's Word instead of returning to commercial fishing.

John ends his writing by saying that he personally witnessed and wrote all these things down. We know that his testimony is true.

Blessings. Have a great day.

CHAPTER SIX

Acts of the Apostles

Day One Hundred Eighty-Two

Acts 1:1–11

Hello Lucas,

After Jesus was resurrected, He showed Himself alive to many people over a period of forty days, even a crowd of five hundred at one time. He spoke about the kingdom of God and showed undeniable proof that He was alive. He came to earth to speak the words of God, pay the price for our sins, and show Himself alive. Now, He was going to return to His Father's side and represent us before God.

Jesus had promised not to leave His followers alone, so He told them to stay in Jerusalem and wait for the coming of the Holy Spirit. Then He was taken up in the clouds to heaven. While His followers watched intently, two angels appeared and said, "This same Jesus . . . will come back in the same way you have seen him go into heaven."

From this we see three things:

1. Jesus is now in heaven representing you before the Father.
2. He sent the Holy Spirit to help you.
3. The "sign" of Jesus's return is when He returns in the clouds for all to see.

Lucas, these promises are yours!

Blessings. Have a great day.

Day One Hundred Eighty-Three

Acts 1:12–26

Hello Lucas,

The eleven disciples went to Jerusalem as Jesus had commanded. In total, about 120 believers joined together in constant prayer, waiting for the promised Holy Spirit to come. I'm sure many questions ran through their minds as they waited for the Holy Spirit to come:

1. Will He look like a person or a spirit?
2. Will it be obvious when He comes?
3. Will He help us the way that Jesus did?
4. What did Jesus mean, "You will receive power when [He] comes on you?"

These are all valid questions for you to consider. Why? Because Jesus promised that God would send His Holy Spirit to all who obey Him. Within ten days, the disciples would have all their questions answered.

When you gave your life to Jesus, you were baptized outwardly in water. God wants to baptize you inside with His Holy Spirit and power. Set special time aside, like the disciples did, to pray until the Holy Spirit baptizes you inwardly. What could that look like when it happens? Tomorrow, chapter two will show us.

Blessings. Have a great day.

Day One Hundred Eighty-Four

Acts 2:1–13

Hello Lucas,

On the very day that the Jewish festival of Pentecost started (their fall harvest celebration), the Holy Spirit came to the believers who were waiting and praying. Here is what it looked like:

1. The room was filled with the sound of a hurricane-force wind.
2. A flame of fire separated and rested on each person without burning them.
3. The Holy Spirit came and filled each person inside like a rushing river.
4. Each person began praising God in different languages that they had not previously learned.

Crowds from at least sixteen countries had arrived at the festival, and they heard the noise coming from the prayer house. They were amazed to hear locals praising God in all of the different foreign languages and asked each other, "What does this mean?" Some of the onlookers made fun of them, saying, "They have had too much wine."

See how the Holy Spirit captured everyone's attention with His dramatic entrance? He also filled the believers with a special power to boldly preach and harvest souls for the kingdom of God.

Lucas, God can do the same thing for you. Remember, when God does powerful spiritual things in your life, others who have not experienced it may either deny its validity or make fun of you. This is simply because they do not understand what is going on. Earlier, Jesus addressed their type of mentality, "You are in error because you do not know the Scriptures or the power of God" (Matthew 22:29).

Blessings. Have a great day.

Day One Hundred Eighty-Five

Acts 2:14–41

Hello Lucas,

The disciples stepped out, and Peter addressed the crowd, saying that no one was drunk, but that this is what God promised through the prophet Joel: "In the last days, God says, I will pour out my Spirit on all people." Then he boldly told them about the death and resurrection of Jesus, proving from scripture that it was God's plan.

Seeing that their nation had killed the Messiah, the people asked, "What shall we do?"

Peter replied, "Repent and be baptized . . . for the forgiveness of your sins. And you will receive the gift of the Holy Spirit."

Notice, fifty days earlier, the disciples were afraid for their lives and went into hiding, and Peter even denied knowing Jesus. Now they are openly preaching about Jesus, and around three thousand believed and were baptized at the same time. What made the difference, and what gave them boldness?

Jesus promised you, "You w ll receive power when the Holy Spirit comes on you." This is the power that makes you bold enough to tell others about Jesus. It is the power that causes their hearts to turn from sin and accept Him.

Blessings. Have a great day.

Day One Hundred Eighty-Six

Acts 2:42–47

Hello Lucas,

When the Holy Spirit came, the church exploded in a single day. The believers received power and spiritual gifts to boldly reach others for God. It was God's spiritual "shock and awe" campaign. The community was in awe as the apostles performed miracles and healings just like Jesus had. All the believers, both new and old, joined together, eating and fellowshipping in each other's homes. If someone had a legitimate need, the others would sell possessions to help them. Every day, they met together and worshipped in the temple courts while the apostles taught them. The community looked favorably on them, and each day, more people accepted Jesus.

Notice how the Holy Spirit gave the believers three things to help them:

1. Inner power, strength, and inspiration to speak the truth boldly
2. Gifts (foreign languages and healings) to grab the attention of the lost
3. Fruit of the Spirit (love for others, joy, peace, kindness, etc.)

This same Holy Spirit power and fellowship is yours; just ask and God will increase it in you.

Blessings. Have a great day.

Day One Hundred Eighty-Seven

Acts 3:1–10

Hello Lucas,

One day, Peter and John were going to the temple and saw a beggar there who was paralyzed from birth. Peter said, "Look at us! . . . In the name of Jesus Christ of Nazareth, walk." Then as he took the man by the hand, the man's ankles became strong, and he jumped to his feet. He went with them into to the temple courts jumping and praising God. All the people recognized him and were amazed. The book of Acts shows us how the Holy Spirit helped believers to minister powerfully just like Jesus.

People often ask, "Why doesn't God do that today?"

He does!

Several years ago, I was preaching the Gospel to a previously unreached people group, the Bugun tribe in the Himalayas, between China and India. Afterward, the people carried a five-year-old girl to me for prayer.

"From birth she has been paralyzed" they said.

When I prayed for her in the name of Jesus, she began to walk, and as a result, many accepted Jesus. Jesus is alive, and His Holy Spirit is still working like this through believers all around the world!

Blessings. Have a great day.

Day One Hundred Eighty-Eight

Acts 3:11–26

Hello Lucas,

When the paralyzed man was healed, all the people came running to see. Then Peter began to preach to them. What did he say?

1. Out of ignorance you crucified Jesus, but God raised Him from the dead.
2. God foretold that Jesus would suffer.
3. Faith in Jesus's name healed the man.
4. Repent and turn to God so your sins may be wiped away.
5. God sent Jesus to turn you from sin.
6. If you won't listen, you will be cut off from God.

Here we see the salvation message that the disciples gave:

1. Our sins separated us from God.
2. Repent of our sins and turn to God.
3. Have faith in Jesus (who He is, how He paid for our sins, and all He taught).
4. God will cleanse us and give us His Holy Spirit and eternal life with Him.
5. If we reject this, hell awaits us.

This is the message that has saved souls for thousands of years. You do not have to create a new message that pleases people. If you speak this same truth, many more will truly be saved.

Blessings. Have a great day.

Day One Hundred Eighty-Nine

Acts 4:1–22

Hello Lucas,

After hearing Peter's message, the group of new believers grew to about five thousand men and their families. The religious leaders were upset that the disciples were speaking about Jesus's resurrection, so they arrested Peter and John.

When questioned before the religious council, Peter said, "It is by the name of Jesus Christ of Nazareth, whom you crucified but whom God raised from the dead, that this man stands before you healed."

After interviewing the lame man, they could not deny the miracle, because he had been lame for forty years. All the people were praising God, so the leaders could not punish Peter and John. Then they made threats and commanded them not to speak or teach at all in the name of Jesus.

Peter boldly replied, "Which is right in God's eyes: to listen to you, or to him? You be the judges!"

Can you see the Holy Spirit at work? Peter is bold, people are healed, hearts are touched, and many accept Christ. The church is alive, powerful, and growing, just as God intended! Now you can understand why Jesus previously said, "It is for your good that I am going away. . . . But if I go, I will send him [the Holy Spirit] to you" (John 16:7).

Blessings. Have a great day.

Day One Hundred Ninety

Acts 4:23–37

Hello Lucas,

When Peter and John were released, they went back and told the others all that happened and how they were threatened. Everyone prayed for more power, boldness, and miracles so that they could openly preach the truth. God responded in verse 31: "The place where they were meeting was shaken. And they were all filled with the Holy Spirit and spoke the word of God boldly."

If God had already sent His Holy Spirit and filled the believers, why did they need to be filled again? The answer can be found in Jesus's words: "Rivers of living water will flow from within them" (John 7:38). External events can cause a river to become dry or blocked. The religious leaders used threats and intimidation to stop the Holy Spirit from flowing through Peter and John. God responded by sending a fresh wave of the Holy Spirit to fill and empower the believers again.

Lucas, when you accepted Jesus, He sent His Holy Spirit to live and work within you. Ask Him to baptize you with a greater filling of power and spiritual gifts, and He will. You will also experience times when you feel like the "river" has been dried or blocked. If you ask, God will gladly fill you again to overflowing.

Blessings. Have a great day.

Day One Hundred Ninety-One

Acts 5:1–16

Hello Lucas,

During this time, all of the believers were united in heart and shared everything that they had. Some would even sell land or houses and bring the money to the disciples to help those in need. One man and his wife wanted to look good in front of others, so they sold a plot of land and brought only part of the money to Peter. They lied to him, saying it was the full price. Peter explained that they were not lying to men, but lying to God and testing the Holy Spirit, so both of them died on the spot, "Great fear seized the whole church and all who heard about these events."

The apostles had performed great healings and miracles, and many more men and women believed. In the middle of all the excitement of experiencing God's favor, these two believers, a man and wife, lost their fear and respect for the Lord. They lied to the Holy Spirit, who was in Peter, and God did the unexpected, He killed them. Paul said it this way: "Since, then, we know what it is to fear the Lord, we try to persuade others" (2 Corinthians 5:11).

Just because God calls you His son or friend does not mean that He is no longer Almighty God. If you lose your respect and fear for the Lord, the unexpected could happen to you also.

Blessings. Have a great day.

Day One Hundred Ninety-Two

Acts 5:17–42

Hello Lucas,

As more and more people believed on Jesus, the Jewish religious leaders became jealous and arrested the apostles. That night, an angel let them out of jail and told them to continue preaching at the temple. The leaders were surprised to find them free and preaching, so they arrested them again.

Peter told them directly, "We must obey God rather than human beings! The God of our ancestors raised Jesus from the dead—whom you killed by hanging him on a cross. God exalted him to his own right hand as Prince and Savior."

The leaders were furious and wanted to stone them. Instead, they gave them a severe beating and commanded them to no longer teach in the name of Jesus. The disciples considered it an honor to suffer for the name of Jesus and kept on preaching that Jesus is the Christ.

The good news of Jesus Christ is the message that brings forgiveness and salvation to man. Though Satan does his best to silence it, he cannot. Every day more people are set free by hearing.

Blessings. Have a great day.

Day One Hundred Ninety-Three

Acts 6:1–7

Hello Lucas,

Along with the new church growth came new problems. Some believers were upset that the care for their widows was being neglected. So after praying together, the apostles had seven faithful men selected to oversee the responsibility. Everyone was pleased, and the church grew more, even a large number of priests believed in Jesus.

Notice how Satan fought each of the things that sustained this great church growth and revival:

1. When the Holy Spirit gave the believers power to boldly preach the Gospel, Satan stirred up the religious leaders, who beat them and said, "Do not preach about Jesus!"
2. The believers sincerely loved and cared for each other's needs. So Satan tempted a couple of believers with pride, and they lied about how much money they gave.
3. The believers had complete unity of heart, and Satan tried to cause issues and envy to bring division.

Because the believers spent so much time in prayer, God helped them to overcome each obstacle. You will experience counterattacks from the enemy as well. Your victories and spiritual advancement will meet with spiritual opposition. Bring each of the issues to the Lord in prayer, and nothing will stop you.

Blessings. Have a great day.

Day One Hundred Ninety-Four

Acts 6:8–15

Hello Lucas,

One of the men selected to care for the widows was named Stephen. As he did his simple duties, he also performed great miracles and preached. Some of the Jewish leaders opposed him, but their arguments failed because he was filled with wisdom from the Holy Spirit. So they hired false witnesses and dragged him before the religious council.

Let's look closer at Stephen. He was only appointed to care for the old, widowed believers. While he was faithfully doing that work, the power of the Holy Spirit enabled him to do many miracles and preach just like the apostles. Why were the apostles not jealous? They knew that in God's kingdom, even the smallest position is a powerful spiritual work. That's why earlier they said, "Choose seven men . . . full of the Spirit and wisdom [to help the widows]."

From this you see that it does not matter where you are placed within God's kingdom. You may be in some small ministry position or working as an electrician. If you allow God to fill you with His Holy Spirit, His miraculous power and wisdom will overflow into the lives of those around you.

Blessings. Have a great day.

Day One Hundred Ninety-Five

Acts 7:1–53

Hello Lucas,

While being questioned by the religious council, Stephen did not answer the false charges being spoken about him. Instead, he gave a powerful sermon to the leaders. He told how God had called Abraham and made their Jewish nation from him. He told how God called Moses to deliver them from Egyptian slavery and give them God's covenant. He told how their forefathers rejected Moses, saying: "Who made you ruler and judge over us?"

Then Stephen accused the religious leaders, saying, "Just like your ancestors: You always resist the Holy Spirit! . . . And now you have betrayed and murdered [the Righteous One (Jesus)]—you who have received the law that was given through angels but have not obeyed it."

Jesus had promised that the Holy Spirit would "prove the world to be in the wrong about sin" (John 16:8). Here, we see the Holy Spirit speaking through Stephen, trying to bring the religious leaders to repentance.

Lucas, see how straightforward Steven is speaking? You are not presenting a "seeker-friendly" message. You are presenting the truth. You cannot sugarcoat the Gospel for people to hear. It is not like coffee, where you ask them, "One lump or two?" before serving. You must speak the truth in love, because only truth has the power to set men free.

Blessings. Have a great day.

Day One Hundred Ninety-Six

Acts 7:54–60

Hello Lucas,

When Stephen finished speaking, the religious leaders were furious. They covered their ears, yelled, and dragged him out of the city and stoned him to death. When Stephen preached, the people stoned him, but when Peter preached, three thousand got saved. Does that mean that Stephen failed, and Peter was successful? Let's look closer:

1. Both men were filled with the Holy Spirit and preached as He led them.
2. Both men proved that the prophets were talking about Jesus.
3. Both men told the listeners about their sins so that they could repent.

The message was the same, but the crowds were different; one group listened to the Holy Spirit, the other hardened their hearts and resisted.

As a follower of Jesus, you do not have to make people receive the truth. You are only told to share the Gospel with others, and if you do that, you have been successful, regardless of their response.

Blessings. Have a great day.

Day One Hundred Ninety-Seven

Acts 8:1–25

Hello Lucas,

Attitudes changed in Jerusalem the day that Stephen was stoned. Saul, a religious Jew, took persecution to the next level by going house to house and dragging Christians off to jail. Most of the believers, except the disciples, fled to the surrounding areas. But wherever they went, they preached about Jesus.

Phillip, one of the seven who was chosen to help care for the widows, fled to Samaria. There he performed great miracles, and many believed and were baptized, including a man called "Simon the Sorcerer." The apostles heard about this and went down to help. When Peter laid his hands on the new believers, they received the inner baptism power of the Holy Spirit.

Satan tried to use severe persecution to silence the message of Christ; instead, God used it to fulfill Jesus's command: "Go into all the world and preach the gospel." Now many more were coming to Jesus.

In your life, you will discover that God takes what the enemy meant for evil, and He turns it for good.

Blessings. Have a great day.

Day One Hundred Ninety-Eight

Acts 8:26–40

Hello Lucas,

One day, an angel told Phillip to go to a certain road. On his way, he saw an Ethiopian official sitting in a chariot. Then the Holy Spirit told him to go up to the chariot. When he did, he heard the man reading from the scroll of Isaiah.

"Do you understand what you are reading?" Phillip asked.

"How can I . . . unless someone explains?" the man replied.

From that scripture, Phillip told him the good news about Jesus.

As they traveled along and came near some water, the Ethiopian asked whether he could be baptized. So Phillip baptized him right there, and the man went on his way rejoicing.

Look at these amazing things:

1. God knew that the Ethiopian was ready to believe and sent Phillip to help him understand.
2. Phillip was close enough to God to hear the angel, and as he obeyed, the Holy Spirit showed him the next step.

You should not be surprised that God wants to use you to reach people that are ready for Him. Just stay close enough to Him so that you can be led like Phillip was.

Blessings. Have a great day.

Day One Hundred Ninety-Nine

Acts 9:1–19

Hello Lucas,

Saul, now well-known for killing Christians, went to Damascus to arrest believers. On his way, a bright light from heaven blinded him. After falling off his donkey, he heard Jesus say, "Saul, why do you persecute me?"

Three days later, God sent a believer named Ananias to pray and restore Saul's eyesight, for God had told Ananias, "This man is my chosen instrument to proclaim my name to the Gentiles and their kings and to the people of Israel." After Saul's eyes were opened, he was baptized and renamed Paul.

Notice what Paul later says about himself in a letter he writes to Timothy: "Even though I was once a blasphemer and a persecutor and a violent man, I was shown mercy because I acted in ignorance and unbelief. . . . so that in me, the worst of sinners, Christ Jesus might display his immense patience as an example for those who would believe in him and receive eternal life." (1 Timothy 1:13, 16).

People may look at someone and say, "There is no hope for him" or "He should burn in hell." But from this story you see that God can save even the worst sinner and change their heart.

Blessings. Have a great day.

Day Two Hundred

Acts 9:20–31

Hello Lucas,

Paul immediately began to preach, proving that Jesus is Christ, and many believed. All the people marveled, saying, "Isn't this the man who persecuted Christians?" He was so effective in reaching others that the religious leaders tried to kill him. However, he escaped by being lowered in a basket down the city wall.

When he returned to Jerusalem, the believers were afraid to accept him, so Barnabas took him to the apostles and told of his conversion. Then Paul preached fearlessly until the Jews there plotted to kill him.

Notice what Paul discovered:

1. His previous beliefs and life ambitions were based on faulty "knowledge."
2. Once he found the truth of Jesus, he embraced and proclaimed it.

In life you will meet some people who do not believe in Jesus. They make it their goal to insult you and oppose everything about Him. Don't be offended, they live by faulty knowledge. Just pray that they will meet Jesus and become a powerful force for truth, like Paul did.

Blessings. Have a great day.

Day Two Hundred One

Acts 9:32–43

Hello Lucas,

Now that Paul was saved, the church had a time of peace and growth. Peter went from town to town encouraging the new believers. In the city of Lydia, he healed a paralyzed man, and many turned to the Lord. In a nearby town called Joppa, a woman of God died, so the believers there sent for Peter. When he arrived, he went into the room alone and prayed. Then turning to her, he said, "Tabitha, get up." And she did! Because of this, many believed in the Lord.

Jesus promised us that the Holy Spirit would give us power to be witnesses, and that is what we see happening here. The believers received power to boldly speak and power to perform miracles. Notice how the people responded—"many" came to God.

Today you must ask the question: "Am I speaking the Word of God boldly and seeing miracles? Am I seeing 'many' accept Christ?" If the answer is no, then you must pray until you are filled with the Holy Spirit and power.

Blessings. Have a great day.

Day Two Hundred Two

Acts 10:1–23

Hello Lucas,

God planned for salvation to come to the whole world through the Jewish nation and specifically through Jesus. At first, the disciples only focused on reaching Jews because non-Jews were considered religiously "unclean." Earlier, Jesus had told His followers, "This gospel of the kingdom will be preached in the whole world" (Matthew 24:14). God was about to help His followers understand that plan.

An angel appeared to a man named Cornelius, a non-Jewish Roman commander, telling him to invite Peter to his house. At the same time, God gave Peter a dream, saying, "Do not call anything impure that God has made clean." God miraculously brought both of these men together so that Cornelius, a Gentile (non-Jew), could hear the Gospel of Jesus.

God had promised that He would make Jesus "a light for the Gentiles, that my salvation may reach to the ends of the earth" (Isaiah 49:6).

Lucas, it does not matter what nationality a person is or how spiritually unclean he may seem. Jesus paid the price to cleanse all who come to Him, even from the farthest ends of the world.

Blessings. Have a great day.

Day Two Hundred Three

Acts 10:24–48

Hello Lucas,

When Peter arrived Cornelius's house was full, because he had invited his close friends and relatives. They said, "We are all here . . . to listen to everything the Lord has commanded you to tell us."

Peter replied, "I now realize how true it is that God does not show favoritism but accepts from every nation the one who fears him and does what is right." Then He preached clearly the good news about Jesus Christ.

While he was speaking, the Holy Spirit fell on Cornelius and all of his guests who were listening. They began to praise God in different languages, just like the disciples had experienced in Jerusalem. Seeing that God had done this, Peter had the entire household baptized in water also.

The Jewish believers were surprised. They did not know that God would pour out His Holy Spirit on foreigners. It showed that God accepted all who believed in Jesus. Next, Peter would go to Jerusalem and help the Jewish believers there understand what God just did.

Sometimes you won't understand what God is doing in your life. You must be willing to be led into new territory and let Him explain along the way as things play out. He has new and exciting things ahead for you. Things that He has already spoken of in His Word, awaiting your discovery.

Blessings. Have a great day.

Day Two Hundred Four

Acts 11:1–18

Hello Lucas,

The news of Cornelius's conversion spread quickly, so the disciples and all the believers across the region heard that the Gentiles were receiving Jesus. When Peter reached Jerusalem, some of the Jewish believers criticized him for meeting with the "unclean" Gentiles. So he explained to them everything as it happened and how God had sent him to Cornelius's house. When they heard that God poured out His Holy Spirit on the Gentiles, they praised God saying, "So then, even to Gentiles God has granted repentance that leads to life."

Man cannot easily grasp the amazing ways of God; they must be revealed in steps. God explained it this way: "As the heavens are higher than the earth, so are my ways higher than your ways and my thoughts than your thoughts" (Isaiah 55:9).

If your heart is open, God will gladly show you what He wants to accomplish in your life and through you. Like Peter, once you understand, God will help you to patiently explain what He is doing to those who oppose you.

Blessings. Have a great day.

Day Two Hundred Five

Acts 11:19–30

Hello Lucas,

The Jewish believers now understood God's plan to reach all people. Some of them from Crete went to Antioch and spoke to the Greeks about the Lord Jesus, and many believed. So the church in Jerusalem sent Barnabas to help the new believers in Antioch. In verse 24, it says this about Barnabas: "He was a good man, full of the Holy Spirit and faith, and a great number of people were brought to the Lord." Then Barnabas got Paul to help him, and together they spent a whole year teaching the large crowds there.

Look what happened when the church realized that all men could be saved:

1. They were astonished but embraced the truth of it (verse 18).
2. They went out and found foreigners and shared the Gospel with them (verse 20).
3. They sent faithful men to properly train the new believers (verses 22 and 25–26).

The Greeks of Antioch were saved because some believers took a simple step to speak to them about Jesus.

Lucas, take that simple step yourself and see who gets saved today.

Blessings. Have a great day.

Day Two Hundred Six

Acts 12:1–11

Hello Lucas,

As believers grew in their knowledge of the Lord, in love, and in obedience to God, Christianity spread quickly. This did not go on unnoticed by the Jewish religious leaders. In order to slow things down, they turned to one of their strongest allies for help—their regional king, Herod Antipas. Even though Herod was Roman and ruled over the Jews, he supported the Jewish religion, their leaders, and their temple. So he arrested the apostle James and had him executed. Seeing that this pleased the Jews, he arrested and imprisoned Peter also. Once again this seems to be a very dark and difficult time of persecution for the church to walk through.

From this you can see that you will have many miraculous spiritual experiences and mountaintop days. You will also encounter temporary defeats that bring grievous, dark nights for your soul. Do not be discouraged, because God has promised, "Never will I leave you; never will I forsake you" (Hebrews 13:5).

A young Christian girl who survived imprisonment in a concentration camp later said it this way: "There is no pit so deep, that God's love is not deeper still" (Corrie ten Boom).

Blessings. Have a great day.

Day Two Hundred Seven

Acts 12:12–25

Hello Lucas,

While Peter was in prison, many believers gathered in a house to pray for him. That very night, an angel woke Peter up; his chains fell off and each iron gate opened as he followed the angel to freedom. When he arrived at the prayer house, the people couldn't believe that such a difficult prayer could be answered so quickly. They thought that he had been martyred and it was his spirit passing by. But when they opened the door, they realized that their prayers were answered. Peter was alive and standing before them.

In the morning, when Herod could not find Peter, he had the guards executed. In the course of time, God struck down Herod, and the Word of God continued to increase and spread.

Often, people pray not really expecting God to answer their hardest requests, thinking that they are not worthy. But God promised that He is "able to do immeasurably more than all we ask or imagine" (Ephesians 3:20).

Lucas, just ask and believe God for great things so that you can increase and spread His Word to the world around you.

Blessings. Have a great day.

Day Two Hundred Eight

Acts 13:1–12

Hello Lucas,

Among the believers in Antioch, there were five prophets gifted by the Holy Spirit. As they prayed and fasted, the Holy Spirit spoke through them, telling Paul and Barnabas to begin a missionary journey. They agreed, and for two years they traveled about 1,400 miles, often on foot, preaching the Gospel. As they preached across the island nation of Cyprus, a sorcerer named Elymas opposed them. Then the Holy Spirit spoke through Paul and struck Elymas blind. When the people and officials saw this, many of them believed in the Lord.

Notice the work of the Holy Spirit in the lives of the believers:

1. The Holy Spirit spoke through the prophets: "Set apart for me Barnabas and Saul for the work to which I have called them."
2. Paul was filled with the Holy Spirit and told the sorcerer, "You are going to be blind for a time."

Jesus already promised that the Holy Spirit would guide and empower you. Always be willing to let the Holy Spirit do that in your life so that many others can believe in the Lord Jesus.

Blessings. Have a great day.

Day Two Hundred Nine

Acts 13:13–52

Hello Lucas,

At Antioch Pisidian, in modern day Turkey, Paul visited a synagogue (Jewish temple). There he showed from scripture that Jesus was Christ. The people were interested and asked him to speak again. The next week, almost the whole city came to hear his message. When the local Jewish leaders saw this, they became jealous, because they could not draw arge crowds, so they opposed Paul. In verse 46, he replied, "Since you reject [the Word of God] and do not consider yourselves worthy of eternal life, we now turn to the Gentiles." Many of the Gentiles believed, and the Word of God spread through the whole region.

Then the Jewish leaders expelled Paul and his team. Look at their response to being rejected:

1. They were filled with joy and the Holy Spirit.
2. They shook the dust off their feet.
3. They went preaching in a new place.

Satan is always trying to keep people in bondage. He uses fear, intimidation, and persecution. But nothing can stop the powerful Word of God from setting men free as you boldly proclaim it.

Blessings. Have a great day.

Day Two Hundred Ten

Acts 14:1–18

Hello Lucas,

Paul and Barnabas went on to Iconium, Turkey's oldest city. There they spoke so effectively that a large number of Jews and Gentiles believed. Even though God confirmed their message with miracles, some people wanted to stone them, so they fled to the city of Lystra. There they met a man who was lame from birth. As Paul was speaking, he looked at the man and said, "Stand up on your feet!" and the man did! The crowds were amazed and thought Paul and Barnabas were Greek gods and wanted to offer sacrifices to them. Paul could barely stop them saying, "We too are only human, like you. . . . Turn from these worthless things to the living God."

Often, people worship whatever they think up in their own mind. They want God to be just as they imagine He is, instead of loving Him for who He really is.

If you continue to speak the truth of Jesus, God will confirm it by doing miracles within the lives of others. Then some will turn from serving "the God of their own imagination" and find the true and living God.

Blessings. Have a great day.

Day Two Hundred Eleven

Acts 14:19–28

Hello Lucas,

Unbelieving Jews influenced the crowd against Paul, so they stoned him and left him for dead. When the disciples gathered around his body, he miraculously got up and they began their journey home. On their return journey, they revisited all the new believers in each town and appointed leaders. No doubt Paul was cut, swollen, bruised, and in pain, but he continued. Before accepting Christ, he previously killed Christians, but when he got saved, God said, "This man is my chosen instrument. . . . I will show him how much he must suffer for my name."

In 2 Corinthians 11:16–33, Paul describes the things that he suffered from doing ministry:

1. Five different times he was flogged with thirty-nine stripes.
2. Three different times he was beaten with rods.
3. He was stoned and left for dead.
4. Three different times he was shipwrecked.
5. Often he went without food, water, clothes, and sleep.
6. Often he was imprisoned, cold, and naked.

Lucas, after reading this, it's possible that you may never complain about your small struggles. Sometimes you will suffer for the name of Jesus. Like Paul, be faithful through all these things, so that you can help many enter the kingdom of God.

Blessings. Have a great day.

Day Two Hundred Twelve

Acts 15:1–21

Hello Lucas,

Paul and his team returned from their two-year missionary journey and told how many Gentiles had been saved through faith in Jesus. Some argued, saying that the Gentiles must be circumcised and observe the Jewish law in order to be saved. So they met with the apostles and elders in Jerusalem to discuss the issue. After much discussion, Peter reminded them that Cornelius's family was saved by faith and that God filled them with His Holy Spirit.

Then James the brother of Jesus said, "We should not make it difficult for the Gentiles who are turning to God." He suggested they only ask the Gentiles to abstain from food sacrificed to idols, from blood, from strangled meat, and from sexual immorality.

You will meet some people who will try to make you observe Jewish laws and customs and instruct you to abstain from eating certain things. Don't let them put these burdens on you. Paul explained it this way, "Therefore do not let anyone judge you by what you eat or drink, or with regard to a religious festival, a New Moon celebration or a Sabbath day" (Colossians 2:16). However Lucas, do not use your freedom to indulge in fleshly lusts.

Blessings. Have a great day.

Day Two Hundred Thirteen

Acts 15:22–41

Hello Lucas,

After realizing that God did not require the Gentiles to observe Jewish laws and customs, the apostles wrote these things in a letter and had their decision shared with all of the churches.

Sometime later, Paul decided to go on a second missionary trip, but he did not want to take a young man named John Mark. John Mark was the one who got homesick and left early on the last trip. Barnabas wanted to give him a second chance. The disagreement was so strong that Paul and Barnabas parted company. Barnabas took John Mark and headed to Cyprus, and Paul chose Silas and headed toward Syria. While these godly men disagreed about ministry details, they later reconciled, and John Mark eventual y joined Paul in ministry.

At some point, you will disagree with another believer on how ministry is done, but your response will be different than the world's. You will not hate, speak evil of, or try to destroy them. Even though you disagree or go different directions, God's love compels you to attempt to repair the relationship.

Blessings. Have a great day.

Day Two Hundred Fourteen

Acts 16:1–15

Hello Lucas,

Paul began his second missionary outreach, and it lasted over two years as he traveled through Syria, Turkey, and Greece. In Lystra, he met a young Greek-Jewish believer named Timothy, who became a spiritual son and joined their ministry. As they traveled from town to town, they read the apostles' decision about the Gentiles' freedom in Christ, and many were encouraged.

Verses 6–10 explain how the Holy Spirit led them to the right places to preach and kept them from entering other areas. One night, Paul had a vision of a man from Macedonia, Greece, saying "Come . . . help us." From this they knew that God was calling them to preach there, so they went. Because they obeyed the vision, five major cities in Greece received the Gospel.

Jesus has commanded you to share to Gospel to the whole world. Let the Holy Spirit lead you to the right people at the right time so that many more can receive the good news of Jesus.

Blessings. Have a great day.

Day Two Hundred Fifteen

Acts 16:16–40

Hello Lucas,

While in the city of Philippi, Greece, a fortune teller followed Paul and his team around, shouting, "These men are servants of the Most High God, who are telling you the way to be saved."

After several days, Paul got tired of it and cast the evil spirit out of her. When this slave girl's owners saw that they could no longer make money from her fortune telling, they falsely accused Paul and Silas. Both were arrested, beaten, and thrown in jail without a trial. In jail they worshipped the Lord, and an earthquake shook their chains off and opened the doors. When the jailer saw this, he became a follower of Jesus. Upon release, they encouraged the new believers and traveled on.

Interest in the occult, spiritism, fortune telling, ghost tours, and Harry Potter type of things has increased in recent years. All occultic fascinations and practices are merely backdoor entrances into a spiritual world of darkness and demonic activity. Ultimately, all of that can bring bondage, demonic possession, and death. As a believer, you must not take part in these things. Instead, do as Paul did: Bring deliverance to the people and teach those who have become unwittingly bound by these things.

Blessings. Have a great day.

Day Two Hundred Sixteen

Acts 17:1–15

Hello Lucas,

Whenever Paul entered a new city, he usually preached to the Jews first. In Thessalonica, when several accepted Jesus, the jealous Jews started a riot, so Paul and his team went on to Berea. There, the Jews eagerly received the message and many of the Jews and Greeks became believers.

Notice, Jesus was preached in both of the cities, but the response was different. In Thessalonica, the Jews started a riot, but in Berea, they eagerly received. Why the difference? Verse 11 tells us: "Now the Berean Jews were of more noble character than those in Thessalonica, for they . . . examined the Scriptures every day to see if what Paul said was true."

In our society, we have endless "spiritual" teaching around us and on the internet. Everyone thinks they are a theological expert. You should neither quickly accept nor reject all that you hear. Instead, like the Bereans, you must examine the scriptures to see if what they say is true. When you eat fish, you do not swallow the bones. Likewise, when you know the Bible, you only swallow truth. The Holy Spirit will show you in the Word what you must spit out.

Blessings. Have a great day.

Day Two Hundred Seventeen

Acts 17:16–34

Hello Lucas,

While Paul was waiting for his team to arrive in Athens, he was surprised to see idols everywhere. He even found a shrine titled, "TO AN UNKNOWN GOD." So he preached to the people about Jesus, and some of them believed. Look at all the methods that Paul used there:

1. He used the quote printed on their own shrine to tell them Jesus is the "Unknown God."
2. He quoted sayings from their local poets to show that God isn't like a man-made idol.
3. He spoke in the Jewish synagogue and in the open marketplace daily.
4. He spoke to common people, religious leaders, Greek philosophers, and the city council of elders.

Jesus has called you to catch "fish" from the sea of sin. When you go fishing, your goal is to catch fish, so you take along a tackle box full of options. Like Paul, be aware of the culture and people around you, then use every method available to effectively catch people for Jesus. As you fish, the Holy Spirit will help you see the best bait to use.

Blessings. Have a great day.

Day Two Hundred Eighteen

Acts 18:1–17

Hello Lucas,

Paul left Athens and went to Corinth where he met a family that made tents. He worked making tents with them during the week and preached on the weekends. When his team arrived, he devoted all his time to the ministry. When the local Jews rejected his words, he left their meeting and went next door to a Gentile's house. As a result, the Jewish-synagogue ruler and his whole house and many other Corinthian citizens accepted Jesus and were baptized. One night, God gave Paul a vision, saying, "Do not be afraid; keep on speaking. . . . No one is going to attack and harm you, because I have many people in this city." So he stayed there a whole year and a half teaching.

Notice, even though Paul was a highly honored apostle, he labored with his hands while he ministered. Some people approach ministry as a paid profession and refuse to do other work. But Paul left you with a very powerful example to follow. He worked with his hands and used every means possible to reach the lost.

Blessings. Have a great day.

Day Two Hundred Nineteen

Acts 18:18–28

Hello Lucas,

Paul preached in Ephesus, Turkey, then left Priscilla and Aquila, the couple that made tents, behind in Corinth to teach. While they were ministering there, a man named Apollos came to town boldly preaching about Jesus. He knew the scriptures well but mostly about John's water baptism of repentance. Priscilla and Aquila took him into their home and taught him more about the Lord Jesus and about the baptism of the Holy Spirit. Then he went on to Achaia, Greece, and convinced many that Jesus was the Christ.

Apollos was a well-educated believer who had a good knowledge of the scriptures and spoke powerfully, but he still had a few things to learn. When a more mature couple approached him, he was humble and learned great things from them. As a result, he became a powerful apostle. Verse 27–28 says that when he went to Achaia, "he was a great help to those who by grace had believed" and he publicly proved that Jesus was the Christ.

Lucas, always stay humble and teachable so that you can be powerful and effective.

Blessings. Have a great day.

Day Two Hundred Twenty

Acts 19:1–22

Hello Lucas,

Paul began his third missionary trip traveling across Turkey, revisiting the churches and eventually arriving in Ephesus. There he held daily discussions in a public lecture hall and reasoned with everyone about the kingdom of God. This went on for two years until everyone in the province of Asia heard the Word of the Lord. God did great miracles through Paul, and people came, openly confessing their sins. A large number of people who practiced sorcery got saved and burned all of their scrolls, which in total were valued at fifty thousand silver coins.

The local Jews had rejected the Word of God, so Paul left the traditional church building (synagogue). He took the Gospel to the streets by using a local lecture hall (school). In doing so, he was able to reach two million people and establish believers all across Turkey.

As a believer, you may gather with others for fellowship and training in a church building. But like Paul, your most effective ministry may happen as you take His Word and power to the people on the streets.

Blessings. Have a great day.

Day Two Hundred Twenty-One

Act. 19:23–41

Hello Lucas,

For over seven hundred years, the people of Ephesus had been worsh ping a female goddess named Artemis (Diana). Her temple was the pride and centerpiece of cultural activity. Her image, that supposedly fell from heaven, adorned pathway shrines all across the region. An entire union of metal workers prospered by making idols and icons honoring her. When so many people accepted Jesus and turned away from worshipping Artemis, these craftsmen caused a citywide riot, saying, "Paul has convinced and led large numbers of people here in Ephesus and in practically the whole province of Asia. He says that gods made by human hands are no gods at all." This uproar went on for about two hours until the city clerk was able to arrive and disburse the crowds.

Even to this very day, the goddess Artemis (Diana) is no longer worshipped there anymore. Notice, within two short years, Paul, led by God, was able to undo seven hundred years of idolatry.

Around 2002, in the Himalayas, we began our missions. It was documented that the Bugun tribe had never had a single Christian believer. We worked all across that area for many years preaching the Gospel, holding healing festivals, and even building a school among them. Today, 75 percent of their people are Christians. Just like Paul, we know the true and living God and the life-changing power of Jesus Christ.

Blessings. Have a great day.

Day Two Hundred Twenty-Two

Acts 20:1–24

Hello Lucas,

As Paul left Ephesus, the Holy Spirit led him to return to Jerusalem. He ended this third missionary journey by traveling through Greece and Turkey revisiting the churches. In his farewell message, he said, "In every city the Holy Spirit warns me that prison and hardships are facing me [in Jerusalem]." And he tells them, "None of you . . . will ever see me again." Then he described his faithful work among them: "I served the Lord with great humility and with tears and in the midst of severe testing . . . You know that I have not hesitated to preach anything that would be helpful to you but have taught you publicly and from house to house. I have declared to both Jews and Greeks that they must turn to God in repentance and have faith in our Lord Jesus."

Paul said he considered his life worth little in hopes of finishing the work that God had called him to. What was that work? Telling everyone the good news of God's grace. He was so intentional about doing it that everyone around him heard the Gospel.

Do you live intentionally, with purpose? Does your life take back seat so that God's plans are accomplished by you?

Blessings. Have a great day.

Day Two Hundred Twenty-Three

Acts 20:25–38

Hello Lucas,

We have all heard the term "wolf in sheep's clothing." Jesus is the one who actually coined that phrase as he warned about fake, destructive spiritual leaders. Now that Paul is leaving the churches that he established, he instructs the leaders to be faithful "shepherds" and to guard the "sheep" from "savage wolves" that will sneak in. It's hard to imagine that someone would present themselves as a Christian leader for the purpose of destroying followers of Jesus, but it is a reality. They are disguised and living among us, "seeking whom they may devour" (see 1 Peter 5:8).

How do you recognize and avoid fake Christian leaders?

1. Paul tells you to "watch" for them. Their words and lifestyle will tell it all.
2. Paul mentions "the word of his grace." Their words and actions must line up with the Word of God.
3. Jesus said, "By their fruit you will recognize them." Does their life reflect love, joy, peace, patience, gentleness, kindness, meekness, self-control, and faithfulness? Or do they use control, intimidation, fear, manipulation, and sinful lifestyles?

Lucas, that is how you recognize the "wolf."

Blessings. Have a great day.

Day Two Hundred Twenty-Four

Acts. 21:1–16

Hello Lucas,

As Paul was returning to Jerusalem, believers along the way asked him not to go. They gave him prophetic warnings about what he would suffer. Verse 11 tells us about a highly respected prophet named Agabus: "He took Paul's belt, tied his own hands and feet with it and said . . . 'In this way the Jewish leaders in Jerusalem will bind the owner of this belt and will hand him over to the Gentiles.' " Paul knew that the Holy Spirit told him to go to Jerusalem, and the prophets knew the Holy Spirit said Paul would suffer if he went. The people thought the prophecies meant, "Don't go," but Paul knew that they were only a heads-up of what he would be facing ahead.

You may also encounter believers who will give you "prophetic words." What do you do when someone says, "The Lord told me to tell you to do this or that"? Just tell that person that you will take it to the Lord in prayer. Like Paul, you must listen to and obey the inner leading and voice of the Holy Spirit for yourself. Then, when a "prophet" speaks to you, the Holy Spirit will show you how it applies to your situation. Take it to the Lord and do as He leads. Don't be gullible and believe every "prophecy" thrown at you.

Blessings. Have a great day.

Day Two Hundred Twenty-Five

Acts 21:17–40

Hello Lucas,

When Paul and his team arrived in Jerusalem, they met with the apostles and elders, who were happy to hear that many Gentiles had accepted Christ. They said, "thousands of Jews have believed." A few days later, some Jews falsely accused Paul of defiling the temple and speaking against the Jewish people and against the law of Moses. Immediately, the crowd locked the temple and started a citywide riot. They beat Paul without a trial and were going to stone him, but a Roman commander passing by intervened. Binding him with chains, he ordered that Paul be taken into custody.

All the prophetic words that Paul had received were now being fulfilled. As Agabus the prophet said, he was bound, and the Jews handed him over to the Gentiles. Paul had traveled ten thousand miles, freely preaching the Gospel. Now he would be in chains preaching the Gospel.

If your situation goes from good to bad, will you still be willing to tell others about Jesus?

Blessings. Have a great day.

Day Two Hundred Twenty-Six

Acts 22:1–21

Hello Lucas,

Before being taken away, Paul was allowed to address the rioting crowd. He told them that he had been a devout follower of Judaism who previously persecuted Christians. He explained that Jesus appeared and spoke to him, and because of that, he believed on Jesus and was baptized in water. Then he said, "When I returned to Jerusalem and was praying at the temple, I fell into a trance and saw the Lord speaking to me. . . . 'Leave Jerusalem immediately, because the people here will not accept your testimony about me. . . . I will send you far away to the Gentiles.' " When the crowd heard this, they rioted again.

One of the most effective ways to introduce others to Jesus is by telling your story (testimony): how your old life was, how you met Jesus, and how things have changed. Like Paul, you will find that some people will not accept your testimony. They don't want to change, and they're angry that you did. Keep telling your story; some who are empty, lost, and hungry will find Jesus because of it.

Blessings. Have a great day.

Day Two Hundred Twenty-Seven

Acts 22:22–30

Hello Lucas,

After Paul spoke, the people shouted, "Rid the earth of him! He's not fit to live!" It seems strange that people respond violently to a message of peace and love. In the world, if someone delivers a good speech or good acting performance, the crowd applauds and gives awards.

Here are the cities that violently opposed Paul's preaching, and here's how they treated him:

1. Damascus, Jerusalem, and Iconium: They plotted to kill him.
2. Pisidian Antioch: They persecuted him.
3. Lystra: They stoned him.
4. Philippi: They flogged and imprisoned him.
5. Thessalonica, Ephesus, and Berea: Crowds stirred up citywide riots.

Paul explained their response this way, "We preach Christ crucified: a stumbling block to Jews and foolishness to Gentiles" (1 Corinthians 1:23).

In the kingdom of God, success is not defined by the audience's response but by the fact that you obediently spoke the Gospel message: All men can have peace with God through Jesus. Many years ago, the Lord told me, "Success can be defined in one word: obedience."

Blessings. Have a great day.

Day Two Hundred Twenty-Eight

Acts 23:1–11

Hello Lucas,

Seeing the crowd's violent reaction, the commander took Paul away to beat and interrogate him. But learning of Paul's Roman citizenship and rights, he instead set an inquiry for the next day. The Jewish leaders and priests brought all kinds of charges against Paul. He was allowed to give his defense, and half of the people supported him, and the other half opposed him. They disagreed so violently that the soldiers had to forcefully rescue Paul and put him in protective custody. The commander's report concluded: "There was no charge against him that deserved death or imprisonment." At night, the Lord stood by Paul and said, "As you have testified about me in Jerusalem, so you must also testify in Rome."

God wants all men to be saved. He was using Paul's unjust situation to tell rulers, leaders, and eventually Nero, ruler of the whole Roman Empire, about Jesus.

God arranges your life situations so that you can meet both servants and leaders. Continue to do your part by sharing the love of Jesus as you meet them.

Blessings. Have a great day.

Day Two Hundred Twenty-Nine

Acts 23:12–35

Hello Lucas,

While Paul was in custody, a group of forty Jews took a vow not to eat until they had killed him. When his relatives found out, they told the commander about the plot. He put together a detachment of seventy calvary, two hundred soldiers, and two hundred spearmen to escort Paul to Felix, the governor of Judea. After arriving safely, he was put in protective custody until his accusers could arrive.

Paul had completed three missionary journeys, which lasted around nine years and covered over ten thousand miles. Now he was beginning another one. This one was planned solely by God and would look different than the earlier ones. Even though Paul was a prisoner the whole time, it was nonetheless his fourth missionary journey. For four years he would give his testimony and preach the Gospel of Jesus Christ, this time to kings and rulers. When Paul first got saved, the Lord said, "This man is my chosen instrument to proclaim my name to the Gentiles and their kings."

Lucas, no one's life is an accident. Like Paul, you were created and chosen by God for a destiny. It is waiting for you to discover and live.

Blessings. Have a great day.

Day Two Hundred Thirty

Acts 24:1–21

Hello Lucas,

After five days, the Jews brought a famous lawyer and presented charges against Paul, accusing him of stirring up nationwide riots and defiling the temple. After they finished, Paul refuted each accusation, showing that there was no supporting evidence. Then he seized the opportunity to present his faith and explained the following:

1. I worship the God of our fathers.
2. I am a follower of the Way (Jesus).
3. I agree with the law and prophets.
4. I believe there will be a resurrection of the righteous and the wicked.

He exposed their motive against him: "It is concerning the resurrection of the dead that I am on trial before you today" (saying that God resurrected Jesus).

Paul knew that his imprisonment and trial was a divine opportunity to share the Gospel of Jesus Christ with political leaders. So he shifted the conversation right to that point.

Several years ago, I had a man come and look at an apartment that I had for rent. He was a big guy that looked like a lumberjack—thick, long beard and all. After a few minutes, I realized that God had brought him to hear the good news of Jesus, not to rent my apartment. As I shifted the conversation, he began to share personal problems and started to tear up. All along, he kept saying, "I don't know why I'm sharing these things; I don't do that. I don't know why I'm crying; I don't do that." The Holy Spirit was working on him, and I was able to share the Gospel and pray with him before he left.

Lucas, some of life's conversations and situations are really divine opportunities set up by God. Smoothly shift the topic to the Gospel and see what happens.

Blessings. Have a great day.

Day Two Hundred Thirty-One

Acts 24:22–27

Hello Lucas,

After hearing Paul's defense, Felix, the governor, dismissed everyone, saying, "When the commander comes . . . I will decide your case." Felix knew that Paul was innocent, but because he loved money, he kept Paul locked up for two more years, hoping to receive a bribe. He was interested in Paul's message and would often have him brought in to talk One time, Felix and his wife, who was Jewish, were listening to Paul talk about having faith in Jesus. As he spoke of self-control, righteousness, and the judgment to come, Felix became nervous and dismissed him.

Notice the message that Paul gave:
1. We must have faith in Jesus.
2. We need to live self-controlled and righteous lives.
3. There is a day where each person will stand before God to be judged.

That simple message has changed the hearts of millions for the past two thousand years. You can change your generation by speaking that same message. All must repent to God and have faith in Jesus.

Blessings. Have a great day.

Day Two Hundred Thirty-Two

Acts 25:1–12

Hello Lucas,

After two years, Felix was called to Rome, and a new governor, Porcius Festus, succeeded him. Immediately, the Jews asked that Paul stand trial in Jerusalem; they were secretly planning to kill him. Festus needed to gain some local acceptance in order to strengthen and maintain his peaceful rule. So after holding a brief hearing, he asked Paul if he would be willing to stand trial in Jerusalem. Paul knew that the Jews only wanted to kill him along the way, so he requested to stand trial before Nero in Rome. Since Paul was also a Roman citizen, his appeal was granted.

Governor's Felix and Festus wanted to use Paul's situation to gain political popularity. The Jewish leaders wanted to kill Paul in order to keep their religious popularity.

Lucas, the world may try to use you to advance their agendas, but they are only playing into God's hands. He uses their plans to accomplish His agenda. "Many are the plans in a person's heart, but it is the LORD's purpose that prevails" (Proverbs 19:21). President Ulysses S. Grant said it this way: "Man proposes, and God disposes. There are but few important events in the affairs of men brought about by their own choice."

Blessings. Have a great day.

Day Two Hundred Thirty-Three

Acts 25:13–27

Hello Lucas,

A few days later, the king of Judea, King Agrippa, arrived with his wife to welcome Governor Festus to his new appointment. During their stay, Festus discussed Paul's case with them. He said, "I did not delay the case, but convened the court the next day and ordered the man to be brought in. When his accusers got up to speak, they did not charge him with any of the crimes I had expected. Instead, they had some points of dispute with him about their own religion and about a dead man named Jesus who Paul claimed was alive. . . . I found he had done nothing deserving of death."

Agrippa was interested, so the next day, they held an inquiry. King Agrippa, Festus, and all the city officials attended, eager to hear Paul's story.

The Jewish religious leaders were trying their best to silence Paul so he could not share the Gospel, but instead, we see God arranging an audience of the most important government officials, who were eager to listen.

In many countries, it is illegal to have a Bible or to preach about Jesus. In 2018, I was banned from India for preaching the Gospel. As a result, God arranged other ways for me to minister to the people of India. I am reaching more now than I did in the previous twenty years. God's arrangements are best, and Satan cannot stop them.

Blessings. Have a great day.

Day Two Hundred Thirty-Four

Acts 26:1–16

Hello Lucas,

Paul presented his own case, saying that he was raised as a devout Jew and served as a religious leader alongside the ones who were now accusing him. He explained that he opposed the name of Jesus by persecuting and killing Christians and trying to get them to renounce their faith. But then Jesus, whom he was opposing, appeared and spoke to him.

Imagine that you believed something to be a certain way. You staked your whole future and way of life on it like Paul did, then you found out that you were mistaken.

Many years ago, before GPS, I took a wrong turn and traveled in the wrong direction for thirty minutes. Although I was going in the wrong direction, it was very hard to admit. I struggled to do that 180º turn and didn't want to lose all that ground that I had covered. However, I made the necessary turn and eventually arrived at my proper destination. I have seen many Hindus and Buddhists who opposed God also turn and gladly accept Him.

In this passage, Paul is offering that same turn-around opportunity to the rulers as he stands trial and tells his story.

Blessings. Have a great day.

Day Two Hundred Thirty-Five

Acts 26:17–32

Hello Lucas,

During his defense, Paul said that God called him to "turn [people] from darkness to light, and from the power of Satan to God, so that they may receive forgiveness of sins and a place among those who are sanctified by faith in [Jesus]."

This is the message that Paul preached everywhere:

1. People should repent, turn to God, and prove their sincerity by changing.
2. The prophets foretold that Christ would suffer and then be the first to rise from the dead and proclaim light to both the Jews and Gentiles.

Since King Agrippa was sympathetic to the Jewish faith and familiar with the scriptures, Paul told him directly, "I know you [believe the prophets]."

Then King Agrippa and all the other officials left, saying, "This man is not doing anything that deserves death or imprisonment."

The King of heaven came to earth, and the kings of the earth rejected Him. God sent Paul to open their eyes so they could understand. If you do like Paul did, no one can say, "I never heard."

Blessings. Have a great day.

Day Two Hundred Thirty-Six

Acts 27:1–26

Hello Lucas,

Paul's appeal to present his case before Caesar was honored. He was put under guard and loaded onto a ship bound for Rome. He was also given limited liberties, and some of his friends were allowed to accompany him. Along the way, they encountered a hurricane and had to fasten ropes under the ship just to hold it together. The next day, they had to throw everything overboard. For many days, they didn't even see the sun or moon. After going a long time without food, Paul encouraged them to eat, saying, "Only the ship will be destroyed. Last night an angel of the God to whom I belong and whom I serve stood beside me and said, 'Do not be afraid, Paul. You must stand trial before Caesar; and God has graciously given you the lives of all who sail with you.' "

Lucas, following God's plan for your life is not always "smooth sailing." He wants to reveal Himself to others through you, and using outstanding events along the way is one of His best methods. Look for God's plan in the storms.

Blessings. Have a great day.

Day Two Hundred Thirty-Seven

Acts 27:27–44

Hello Lucas,

For fourteen days, they went without food while battling the storm, and everyone had given up hope. Before dawn, Paul encouraged them, saying, "Take some food. You need it to survive. Not one of you will lose a single hair from his head." Then after he gave thanks, they all ate.

When daylight came, they saw a beach and decided to run the ship aground. The bow stuck in the sand, and the stern was broken into pieces by the waves. Everyone swam for shore and all 276 passengers reached land safely, just as Paul had said. God had told Paul that he would witness to Caesar and that all the passengers would be saved. Outwardly this seemed impossible, but Paul had great faith and trusted God.

Believing God and His Word instead of external circumstances, even though everyone else gives up hope, is the sign of a mature and productive disciple. "Now faith is confidence in what we hope for and assurance about what we do not see" (Hebrews 11:1).

Blessings. Have a great day.

Day Two Hundred Thirty-Eight

Acts 28:1–16

Hello Lucas,

After safely reaching shore on the island of Malta, the locals made a fire to warm the survivors. While gathering firewood, Paul was bitten by a poisonous viper but suffered no problems. When the islanders saw this, they "said he was a god." The chief official hosted them in his home for three days and told them that his father had dysentery and a fever. When Paul prayed and laid his hands on the sick man, he was healed. Then all who were sick came and were healed. Three months later, after winter passed, they were loaded onto another ship that was headed for Rome. After arriving safely, Paul was allowed to rent a house, and a soldier was appointed to guard him.

Paul said, "This is my gospel, for which I am suffering even to the point of being chained like a criminal. But God's word is not chained" (2 Timothy 2:8–9).

The enemy will use circumstances to tie your hands, but because you love and obey God like Paul did, nothing can stop the Word of God that you speak. It truly is the "unchained Gospel," and that Gospel has the power to change the lives of many.

Blessings. Have a great day.

Day Two Hundred Thirty-Nine

Acts 28:17–31

Hello Lucas,

Three days after arriving in Rome, Paul explained his situation to the Jewish leaders there, so they asked him to explain more about Jesus Christ. A large crowd came to his house to listen as he taught all day about the kingdom of God and showed them where the law of Moses and the Prophets foretold about Jesus. Some were convinced, and others would not believe. For two full years, Paul boldly preached about Jesus and God's kingdom while chained and awaiting his trial before Caesar.

God put Paul in a unique situation where he shared the Gospel with Rome, a city of four million people.

The results were amazing:
1. Some of Caesar's own household were saved.
2. The elite palace guard of ten thousand soldiers heard the Gospel.
3. Many nonbelievers accepted Jesus.
4. The local believers were encouraged and boldly proclaimed the Gospel.
5. The church grew and was strengthened.

Lucas, Jesus chose to build God's kingdom and establish His church, starting with simple and uneducated fishermen. He went on to use people like Paul who were highly educated in the secular and religious ideologies of his day. And in this book of Acts, you see Him using people from every walk of life and social status.

From this you see that the effectiveness of the Gospel is not based upon your own intellect or ability, but solely upon the power of the Holy Spirit working through you. Paul said it this way, "My message and my preaching were not with wise and persuasive words, but with a demonstration of the Spirit's power, so that your faith might not rest on human wisdom, but on God's power" (1 Corinthians 2:4–5).

Just like them, great things will happen as you live a life full of the Holy Spirit and of radical obedience to God. This book of Acts doesn't have to end here, its story can continue with you!

Blessings. Have a great day.

CHAPTER SEVEN

Fairwell Letter to Lucas

Hello Lucas,

You did it! We spent a little over a year going through the teachings of Jesus, and you've grown so much. Don't let this relationship end there. I know that you won't. Move forward by reading the scriptures that follow the book of Acts. My wife and I start in Genesis and read the Bible through. When we finish, we start all over again. Year after year that goes on, and each time the Lord shows us something new and exciting! I do not know when you and I will see each other again, but you will always be in my thoughts and prayers. Never stop hungering for God and never stop growing in Him.

You have entered into a new and amazing life with Jesus Christ. Your spirit has been born again by the Spirit of God. Previously, like all of us, you lived a life of selfish indulgence, fulfilling all kinds of lust and experiencing fleshly pleasures and lacking proper love for others. Your sins and fallen nature moved you along in life. But now all of those past sins have been forgiven. And as they die and fall away from you, your thoughts and actions are undergoing a renovation process. God is removing all of the old things and replacing them with His divine nature and characteristics. Peter said it this way, "His divine power has given us everything we need for a godly life through our knowledge of him who called us by his own glory and goodness. Through these he has given us his very great and precious promises, so that through them you may participate in the divine nature" (2 Peter 1:3–4).

You know what your old nature was like, but in order to fully appreciate the promise of transformation, you must ask the question, "What does the divine nature of God that I am receiving look like?" Paul describes this creative work whereby the Holy Spirit produces the divine nature of God inside of you. "But the fruit of the Spirit is love, joy, peace, forbearance, kindness, goodness, faithfulness, gentleness, and self-control" (Galatians 5:22–23). These beautiful character traits are the very divine essence of God, the Holy DNA of heaven, and are available to you. Imagine that! God not only sent His Son to die for your sins, and that in itself would have been enough, but now His Spirit is living in you, allowing you to experience the same nature that He enjoys. It's like He is saying, "It's really nice up here; come up and join me. This can be yours too!" What a precious promise; you do not have to forever go through life being your "old, bad self."

No doubt by now you are experiencing some of the benefits and outcomes of your spiritually redeemed life. That transformation process will continue throughout your whole lifetime. Here are three powerful tools that the Holy Spirit is using to separate the old from the new in your life:

1. The Blood of Jesus. The Holy Spirit is working within you to make you aware of the things that are sin so that you can deal with them and be free. Often, He uses a gentle inner voice or a touch on your conscience. Learn to cooperate with that. Freely discuss your issues with God and turn from them.

   > If we claim to have fellowship with him and yet walk in the darkness, we lie and do not live out the truth. But if we walk in the light, as he is in the light, we have fellowship with one another, and the blood of Jesus, his Son, purifies us from all sin. If we claim to be without sin, we deceive ourselves and the truth is not in us. If we confess our sins, he is faithful and just and will forgive us our sins and purify us from all unrighteousness. (1 John 1:6–9)

2. The Word of God. The Holy Spirit is always leading you through the truth of God's Word. As He does, your understanding and thinking will turn toward truth and God's way of seeing things. Your thoughts will become clean, clear, and have an eternal and spiritual perspective. Read the Bible daily, and when you do, ask the Holy Spirit to open your understanding. You will notice that certain verses will "jump out" and speak directly to you. At that moment, it is God sharing what is on His heart for you. Jesus said it this way, "Sanctify them by the truth; your word is truth" (John 17:17). "But when he, the Spirit of truth, comes, he will guide you into all the truth" (John 16:13).

3. The Holy Spirit. The Holy Spirit is the active agent and indwelling presence of God. He is your tour guide, your heavenly GPS for spiritual life. Learn to hear His gentle voice and leading. He is sent from God to assist you in every element of your life. He is always led by the truth of God and will never teach you something or ask you to do something that is contrary to God's Word.

If you love me, keep my commands. And I will ask the Father, and he will give you another advocate to help you and be with you forever—the Spirit of truth. The world cannot accept him, because it neither sees him nor knows him. But you know him, for he lives with you and will be in you. (John 14:15–17)

Blessings. Have a great day.

Daniel F. Hurt

Epilogue

Dear Reader,

Thank you for joining Lucas and me as we explored the teachings of Jesus. Maybe you are a new Christian, an older Christian, or simply someone who is a curious spiritual seeker. Maybe a friend or relative gifted you this book, and you accepted their challenge. No matter where you are in your spiritual journey, I'm sure, that like millions of others, you were touched and challenged as Jesus's words helped you discover the very heart of God.

Have you given your life to Jesus Christ yet? Have you made a commitment to take to heart and follow the teachings of Jesus? If you were to die tonight, are you certain that you have eternal life with God? If you are not sure, here is how you can receive Jesus Christ right now:

1. Admit your need. (I am a sinner.)
2. Repent. (Be willing to turn from your sin.)
3. Have faith in Jesus. (Believe that Jesus Christ died for you on the cross and rose from the grave.)
4. Receive Him as Lord and Savior. (Through prayer, invite Jesus Christ to come in and control your life through the Holy Spirit.)

Pray this prayer:

Dear Lord Jesus,
I am a sinner, and I ask for Your forgiveness.
I believe that You died for my sins and rose from the dead.
I turn from my sins and invite You
to come into my heart and life.
I want to trust and follow You
as my Lord and Savior.
In Your name,
amen.

If you prayed that prayer and meant it, you are now cleansed, saved, and born into God's family. I would love to hear that you made that decision. Let me know how this book has affected your life. Send your email to: Danielfhurt@yahoo.com, or visit my website **danielhurtbooks.com.**